LC

The Catholic in Secular Education

The Catholic in Secular Education

by

JAMES M. O'NEILL, LL.D., L.H.D.

Introduction by
GEORGE N. SHUSTER
PRESIDENT OF HUNTER COLLEGE

LONGMANS, GREEN AND CO.
NEW YORK · LONDON · TORONTO
1956

LONGMANS, GREEN AND CO., INC.
55 FIFTH AVENUE, NEW YORK 3

LONGMANS, GREEN AND CO., LTD.
6 & 7 CLIFFORD STREET, LONDON W 1

LONGMANS, GREEN AND CO.
20 CRANFIELD ROAD, TORONTO 16

THE CATHOLIC IN SECULAR EDUCATION

PUBLISHED SIMULTANEOUSLY IN THE DOMINION OF CANADA BY
LONGMANS, GREEN AND CO., TORONTO

FIRST EDITION

LIBRARY OF CONGRESS CATALOG CARD NUMBER 56–8257

Printed in the United States of America

Preface

The words "secular" and "secularism" have different meanings under varying circumstances, and even under identical circumstances sometimes mean different things to different people. In the title of this book, secular refers in general to all types and levels of education which are not administered by religious organizations. While some of the remarks made concerning non-Catholic education in secular institutions would apply to non-Catholic religious education, whenever only such educational institutions or influences are discussed, the reference to them is made specific. Without such specific reference to, for instance, Protestant colleges in the United States, it should be understood that I am not including them in my discussion of Catholics in non-Catholic education. There are relatively few Catholic students or Catholic teachers in Protestant, Jewish, or other types of non-Catholic educational institutions under religious auspices in this country.

This book is designed to give accurate information on the conditions (dangers, handicaps, and favorable opportunities) which confront both Catholic students and Catholic teachers in secular education in the

United States. It is my hope that it will help students and teachers more easily to avoid the dangers, overcome the handicaps, and make the most of favorable opportunities, in their activities in secular institutions.

Of course, I am not discussing the educational doctrines of the Church or trying to persuade more Catholic students to enter secular institutions. I am not attempting to prove any particular thesis. My purpose here is, rather, to bring together in one volume matters of objective fact, dependable reports of illuminating incidents, and the opinions of many experienced Catholic observers of conditions in secular education. Such opinions have been gathered from Catholic teachers and administrators in secular institutions, and from Catholic priests who have had experience as chaplains serving students in non-Catholic schools and colleges.

I hope this book will have some influence in promoting the following:

1. Better training in Catholic religion and history of Catholic students who enter secular education.

2. More awareness on the part of these students *when they enter* of the conditions, the dangers, and the opportunities, especially, for spreading information and understanding to help counteract the widespread misinformation and misunderstanding they will find.

3. More attention, time, and money given specifically to promote (1) and (2) by parents, teachers, pastors, and other counselors.

4. Greatly increased knowledge, and support, of the work of the Newman clubs and Catholic student centers on the college level, and the organization of such a group on every non-Catholic campus that has many Catholic students. A Newman Club under the direction of a carefully chosen chaplain is the most effective agency we have to serve the spiritual needs of the *majority* of future Catholic men and women who will have a college education.

5. Greater understanding, and promotion, of released time, especially on the high school level as a potent agency for helping the 70 per cent of young Catholics who go beyond the elementary schools. Released time, either in the public school buildings (McCollum [1] case to the contrary notwithstanding), or outside of the school buildings (Zorach case),[1] apparently has a great future in spite of the vagaries of the U.S. Supreme Court.

6. A greater number of competent Catholic scholars and teachers on the faculties of non-Catholic institutions, particularly the colleges and universities.

What I say here is based in the first place upon my experience and observation in nearly seven decades in secular education. All of my schooling, my college education, and my postgraduate study were carried on in secular institutions: the country school in District Number 5 in the township of Victor, N.Y.; the Victor High School, Canandaigua Academy (a public high school), Dartmouth College, Harvard Law School, and the University of Chicago Law School. I have spent forty-six years as a teacher in secular education—six in

[1] See pp. 108, 127.

private institutions and forty in public. In these years I taught every grade of education from the first in a country district school to graduate school seminars for doctoral degree candidates in state universities; I have been a teacher in eight states—three in New England and three in the Middle West, as well as in New York and California. I have clearly had at least an opportunity to learn at first hand a great deal about the Catholic student and the Catholic teacher in non-Catholic education. And I have read the publications of, and had personal consultations and correspondence with, many other Catholics thoroughly experienced in secular education. I quote from a number of them with their permission.

The size of the problem of the Catholic in secular education is indicated by the number of young Catholics involved, plus the problem of furnishing them with the religious training and services they need. What is at stake is the religious background of the majority of the future Catholic men and women of America who will have any formal education beyond the elementary school, plus one half of those who have only elementary schooling.

In the various estimates for the decade 1955–1965 that have appeared in the Catholic press, no authority seems to envisage the possibility of the Catholic schools being able to take in a larger percentage of students than in the year just closed. All commentators seem to agree that this will inevitably mean still greater numbers of Catholic children and youth in secular education. As Monsignor McManus, of the Education Department of the National Catholic Welfare Council, has said: "It is no longer sensible to talk about Catholics avoiding secular education." Millions of them can get formal education nowhere else.

The matter of attending to the religious life of the students in the public schools is primarily taken care of by parents and pastors. However, it seems beyond question that in many places the programs commonly referred to as "released time" should be even more widely used than at present, more carefully administered, and much more fully supported. They offer potentially tremendous assistance to busy pastors and parents in seeing to it that the millions of children and youth in public schools are given as nearly as possible the religious training they need. These programs will be discussed at some length in Chapter 6.

There are between eleven hundred and twelve hundred non-Catholic institutions of higher education in this country; over seven hundred of them have Newman clubs or Catholic student centers; about five hundred of these have priests assigned to them as chaplains. I know of no Catholic who has had an opportunity to become familiar with the work of these organizations and their chaplains who is not enthusiastic about their accomplishments with the Catholic students in secular colleges and universities; and I have never known or heard of a non-Catholic administrator or teacher who has objected to their influence. Even the avowed agnostics and atheists who are "against religion" seem not opposed to these student organizations or to the chaplains. However, there are problems, and there are some ways of avoiding, reducing, or solving them which will be taken up in Chapter 7.

I wish to acknowledge the assistance that I have received from many Catholic members of the faculties of secular colleges and universities, and from the many priests who have served in these institutions as chaplains to the Catholic students. A number in both groups, for reasons that seemed good to them, preferred not to have their names mentioned in connection with some of the opinions expressed or incidents cited. Under the circumstances it has seemed best not to mention by name either individuals or institutions, but to refer only to the type of institution, and to give only the principal items in the background and experience of the person reporting. My warmest thanks to all of them for their contributions.

Lakeville, Connecticut
October, 1955   —J. M. O'Neill

Contents

Dedicated to the Memory of

FATHER HENRY CHARLES HENGELL

A Pioneer Chaplain in the Newman Club Movement
University of Wisconsin
1906 – 1936

Introduction

GEORGE N. SHUSTER

Anything "controversial" is held by some observers to have become tabu in American society, but I am for my part persuaded that we have in our history seldom had so many stiff arguments about nearly everything under the sun—politics, art, education, religion, yes, even comic books and cigarettes—as we are now having. Mr. O'Neill has accordingly been as up to date as senators in a discussion on TV. His various books have wrestled boldly with problems growing out of the confrontation of Catholic and non-Catholic in the United States. Perhaps because he taught the art of public speaking for a good many years, he is as wily and resourceful a debater as one is likely to meet. Yet nobody was ever less of a sophist or special pleader. Proud as he is of his heritage and commitments, which are never left in doubt, he is also unfailingly concerned with getting the facts straight. The result is that while those who are on his side of the fence do not always agree with him, the opposition cannot and does not complain of ungentlemanly tactics even while dissenting violently.

In this book Mr. O'Neill deals with a question which may be stated as follows: What measures are being taken to prepare Catholics for their share in the intellectual and professional work of the nation, and what can be said about the adequacy of those measures? As everyone realizes, a Catholic does not believe that religious faith is something you buy casually by the yard when you are so minded. It is a sort of skin which is nearer to you than physical skin. It is truth apprehended, dwelt with, loved, suffered for, if need arises, handed on from generation to generation. Yes, in sober reality, the faith is akin to life itself. On the other hand, there are a great many people in the country who do not feel that way. Many of them believe that other things are more important and interesting than religion, and some find it very boring. There are others who feel quite as strongly about their own faiths, which differ profoundly from that of the Catholic in terms both of tradition and of aspiration. As a result, barriers arise even when there is no conflict.

One result is that Catholics have built up and continue to maintain educational institutions ranging all the way from kindergartens to universities. As might be expected, by far the largest number of young people in attendance at them go to parochial elementary schools—as a matter of fact, more than three-fourths of the total of more than five million. This system unquestionably has its faults, as all educational ventures do, and Mr. O'Neill deals quite candidly with some of them. But it is a very remarkable achievement nevertheless, possibly the most remarkable in the modern history of the Catholic Church, in terms both of organization and of dedicated personnel. These schools are bound to remain with us. None of the critics who profess to wish they were abolished has explained just what steps he would take to bring the demolition about. To begin with, if the critic had his way the taxpayer would be saddled with another debt of astronomical proportions. Then he would perforce end up by employing the same teachers who now serve Catholic schools, as the Communist usurpers of Hungary and Poland have, because no others would be obtainable. And of course, as Mr. O'Neill notes, the first victims of an all-out effort to establish a publicly administered educational monopoly would be the private Protestant schools and colleges.

But the fact is that despite serious overcrowding in Catholic schools, as well as inordinately heavy teaching loads and salaries which are often substandard, the majority of young Catholics attend educational institutions which are not conducted under the auspices of their Church. This is true at all levels, especially those of the high school and the college. Nor is there any expectation that this situation will

change. The authorities on such matters agree that
the current increase of population will inevitably result in larger numbers of Catholic youngsters in "secular" schools. What can be done to insure their spiritual
welfare? It is the same question which Jewish and
Protestant parents are asking about their children.
That interest in and anxiety about the religious training of American youth are growing has been demonstrated by the Religious Education Association beyond
the shadow of a doubt. But if this concern is ever to
get beyond the talking stage, people must learn to put
their heads together, rid themselves of unrealistic prejudices, and find ways of coping with the problem.

Most of what Mr. O'Neill has to say about this cru-
cially important matter has to do with higher education, but his book includes a good chapter about
"release time" in the schools, and about certain Supreme Court decisions affecting it. What the Court
did through the now famous McCollum Decision was
in essence to say that if a class in religion is taught in a
public school building Church and State are felo-
niously conjoined. This was not quite like averring that
if PS. 89 and St. Patrick's Church are in the same
block the danger of contamination is great, but it
almost was. This decision and others undoubtedly
made "release time" instruction more difficult, but did
not abrogate it. More troubling is the fact that under

existing conditions very many youngsters who by all means ought to have religious instruction do not receive any. These are the mentally substandard and potentially delinquent boys and girls who are usually kept out of parochial schools as "bad apples" and whose parents do not take the trouble to enroll them for religious teaching. It seems to me that here is a field of activity, missionary in character if you will, which those concerned with our spiritual welfare ought to cultivate. The youngsters in question give the public schools in not a few congested urban areas 90 per cent of their troubles; and of course these schools cannot teach anything which even indirectly suggests religious motivation.

The situation in the larger "secular" colleges and universities is carefuly described by Mr. O'Neill on the basis of many years of personal experience as well as of the reasoned opinions of others. He makes a number of points which I believe are well taken and which merit widespread study and discussion. First, although teachers who consider religious faith outmoded or untenable can be found on not a few campuses, there are many more who live steadfastly in the light of Protestant, Catholic, and Jewish traditions. These last would be more numerous were it not for the fact that Catholic instructors are almost unbelievably scarce. Not a few explanations of this phenomenon have been offered. No doubt the best answer is that a price must be paid for every privilege. The households of ministers and rabbis have been the cradles of scholars. But the Catholic priest, whose celibacy insures heroic dedication to the Church and often inspiring sanctity, can found no such household. He can only seek to discover other gifted young men who will emulate his example. There can be no doubt that from the religious point of view the sacrifice is noble and rewarding. But it must be compensated for in terms of more mundane academic achievement.

It follows that, in order to uphold religious interests in a prevailingly indifferent academic environment, priests must be enlisted. Indeed they are not found wanting in a great number of places. The Newman Clubs, which band Catholic students together for the safeguarding and intensification of religious life on the campus, have rendered yeoman service; and every educator familiar with developments will endorse what Mr. O'Neill says about them. Yet obviously these Clubs need to be established where they do not now exist, and to be strengthened where they do. At some of our major universities, for example, institutes comparable with Campion House at Oxford might well be founded. The major difficulty is a serious shortage of qualified priests who can be spared for this work. There are also economic problems. It goes without saying that Protestants and Jews are handicapped in like manner.

I think the reader of this book will put it down persuaded that American education has not signed a pact with the devil against religion. The average adult member of any faculty is fully aware of how tenuous the straws are to which many young people cling. He also knows that many of them come to the college or the university poorly prepared. In particular, how shall a young man attempt to find the Lord God in a world so full of a number of things that His voice may seem no louder than a stadium full of football fans? Education has no easy answer for such a question or for many another. Mr. O'Neill's book also has no easy answers to suggest. That is one reason why it is an educated book.

1

The Present Situation

The Official Catholic Directory for 1955 [1] gives the following figures for the enrollment in Catholic schools in the United States, including Alaska and Hawaii, for the school year 1954–55:

Parochial elementary schools	3,253,608	
Private Catholic elementary schools	95,685	
		3,349,293
Diocesan and parochial high schools	398,192	
Private Catholic high schools	241,415	
		639,607
Total in schools		3,988,900
Catholic colleges and universities		219,706
Total for all		4,208,606

According to a report [2] from the annual meeting of the Diocesan Directors of the Confraternity of Christian Doctrine in San Francisco, only 50 per cent of Catholic children are in Catholic elementary schools,

---

[1] (New York: P. J. Kenedy & Sons, 1955), General summary, p. 1–2.
[2] *Catholic Transcript* (Hartford), August 11, 1955.

and only 30 per cent of Catholic high school pupils in Catholic high schools. Archbishop Vehr of Denver reported to the annual meeting of the Newman Club chaplains in Boulder, Colorado, in August, 1955, that in 1954–55 there were 385,000 Catholic students in non-Catholic colleges and universities. On the basis of these statements, the figures for the enrollment of Catholics in non-Catholic education in the United States are:

Elementary schools	3,349,293
High schools	1,492,414
Colleges and universities	385,000
Total	5,226,707

If the size of the total number of students in Catholic education is subtracted from this total, we have:

5,226,707
4,208,606
1,018,101

as the size of the majority enrolled in non-Catholic education.

All available evidence indicates that these *numbers* will increase each year in the foreseeable future, and all commentators in the Catholic press seem to agree that, therefore, the task of maintaining the present level of buildings, equipment, and personnel for the current *proportion* of the Catholic students in Catholic schools presents tremendous problems. No one seems to regard more than this as a possibility in the next decade. Not only is public education at present furnishing the only schooling most Catholics will ever know, but this situation will probably continue indefinitely. Further, public education will doubtless continue indefinitely to be the only education of the overwhelming majority of all Americans. It seems to follow that any person interested in the future of America should be deeply interested in the objectives, programs, and conditions of public education.

The situation revealed by these facts should receive more attention than American Catholics have been giving to it in the past. The entire Catholic population of the country should be made aware of the facts in regard to the education, including the religious education, of all the Catholic children and youth in America. The majority of the Catholics who are being educated in the public schools of America should get as much attention from the Church as the minority who are now in Catholic schools.

Further, our non-Catholic fellow citizens should be made aware of the Catholic interest in public education, which interest should be universal, constant, and well informed. Particularly, non-Catholic Americans should be courteously provided with accurate information on both the extent and the quality of the contribution of the Catholic schools to our society in the intellectual development and the moral and physical health of the millions of young Americans being prepared for adult American life. If this job is to be well done, Catholics will have to invest competent attention, time, and money in doing it. I believe it will be cordially and sincerely welcomed by the great majority of non-Catholic Americans. Perhaps the greatest drawback the Church and American Catholics have is the smug satisfaction with everything Catholic, and the resulting lack of contact with their non-Catholic fellow citizens, on the part of a small, but vocal and influential, minority of Catholics—the impact on Catholicism in America of what Father Mcguire of the Wayne University Newman Club called the "ghetto mentality."

The contribution that the Catholic educational system makes to American taxpayers should be better known, not only to Catholics, but to Americans of every religion and of none. According to the United States Office of Education,[3] the average cost per pupil per year (1954–1955) in 84 school systems in cities with a population of 100,000 or more was $298; in 99 school systems in cities of population between 25,000 and 100,000, the cost per pupil per year was on the

[3] *Current Expenditures per Pupil in Public School Systems* (U.S. Department of Health, Education and Welfare, Circulars no. 436 and 438 [Washington, D.C., March, 1955]), p. 4 in both.

average $246; the average cost per pupil per year in 154 city school systems in cities with a population between 10,000 and 25,000 was $233; in 118 city school systems in cities with the population between 2,500 and 10,000, the average cost per pupil per year was $246. Taking the average of the cost per pupil per year in the 272 school systems of the smaller cities, we get an average of $239.50 per year per pupil. Taking the average of the cost per pupil in the 183 larger school systems, we get an average of $272 per pupil per year. Then, to get a proportional cost per pupil per year for the whole country, we take two times the $272 and three times the $239.50, since 183:272 is substantially 2:3. These totals together equal $1,262.50 and one fifth of that amount is $252.50.

Multiplying the 3,988,900 (the number of students in Catholic elementary and high schools reported by the *Catholic Directory*) by $252.50 (the approximate average cost per pupil per year in the 455 school systems of various sizes reported by the United States Office of Education), we get a total of $1,007,197,250 as the approximate amount of money which the Catholic elementary and high schools save to the taxpayers of the United States each year under present conditions.

Perhaps a few area figures will help to make this situation even more plain. According to a news story in the *Catholic Transcript* [4] the Catholic educational system of the State of Connecticut saves Connecticut taxpayers at the present time $15,500,000 per year. The *Boston Pilot* [5] reported that the Catholic schools saved the taxpayers supporting the city public schools in the archdiocese of Boston an average of $5.90 per $1,000 of valuation which would, in the city, bring the present school tax, averaging $15.51 per $1,000, to an average of $21.42 per $1,000. The report showed that the Catholic educational system saved the individual taxpayers supporting the town public schools in the archdiocese an average of $3.72 per $1,000 of valuation, which would bring the current tax at that time, $16.33 per $1,000, up to $20.55 per $1,000.

The *Pilot* later reported [6] that in the diocese of Worcester alone, by using the same formula of figures, it was found that the Catholic educational system of that diocese was saving the taxpayers $4,908,900 per year.

On the basis of the common school year of 180 days, the Catholic elementary and high schools save the American taxpayer $5,595,540.00 each school day of the school year.

I do not have comparable figures for the other kinds of religious day schools in this country, but we apparently have Jewish, Lutheran, Baptist, Presbyterian,

[4] (Hartford), January 3, 1955.
[5] The diocesan paper of Boston, Mass., September 4, 1954.
[6] March 9, 1955.

Episcopalian, and probably others. If the desire *for universal public education* expressed in the pamphlet *Public Education and the Future of America*[7] is ever realized, the costs borne at present by *all* religious schools and *all* private schools would be added to the present burdens of the taxpayers. According to American constitutions and traditions and the ordinary decencies of our pluralistic society, all would get essentially the same treatment. The depressing and leveling effect of universal public education would obliterate many healthy differences beside those implicit in freedom of religion and freedom of education.

In relation to this aspect of our subject everyone should know that the charge sometimes made by such propagandists as Mr. Blanshard, Professor Nichols, Bishop Oxnam, and others that Catholic authorities are seeking *special privileges* from the government is wholly false. I have seen many expressions of this accusation, but have never found it accompanied by even an attempt at proof. So far as I have been able to discover, no responsible American Catholic has ever advocated any rights or privileges for the Catholic Church, the Catholic schools, or the Catholics of the United States that did not include the other religious groups. And Catholic school authorities have not in

[7] Published by the Educational Policies Commission, Washington: National Education Association and the American Association of School Administrators, 1955. See pp. 42ff.

recent decades, *if ever*, asked for (and probably would not accept if it were offered) total support, or support equal to that of the public schools, from public funds.

In the opinion of those who are best acquainted with the situation, the chief reasons why such large numbers of Catholic students are in secular colleges are four:

1. Four years in a secular college costs so much less. Free, or very low, tuition is the great attraction of the public colleges; scholarships also play a part. In the private secular colleges the scholarships are more potent attractions than lower tuition. In both types of secular institutions the availability (real or supposed) of opportunities to earn money while in college is also effective.

2. Some fields of study (agriculture, engineering, veterinary science, and even law and medicine in parts of the country) are not often to be found in Catholic institutions; sometimes there are individual departments or particular courses found in some secular institutions that attract the student.

3. Simple proximity, the fact that the student can go home frequently at small cost in time or money, is sometimes the determining reason.

4. Relative freedom to live as he pleases, with little or no supervision, the imagined opportunity to have a very good time, to gain social prestige, to make

friends who will be useful in business or professional life, also attract students.

It appears that the best-informed commentators believe that these reasons are operative in a descending number of cases in the order given. Money is the main consideration, social advantage the least important.

2

The Foreseeable Future

There are three prophecies concerning the foreseeable future that can probably be made with complete confidence: (a) religious education, specifically in Catholic elementary and high schools, will continue to function until American freedom is quite extinguished and we become the subjects of a totalitarian dictator or party; (b) the Catholic school system will expand considerably in the next decade—and after; (c) the majority of Catholic children and youth will continue to get their formal education in non-Catholic institutions from the elementary school through the colleges and universities.

Those who look forward to the ending of religious education in the United States are, in all probability, going to be disappointed. So long as our country maintains elementary civil liberties, freedom of religion and of education, there can be no governmental compulsion in favor of the totalitarian concept of public schools only for all American children. In opposition to compulsory public education, the substantially unanimous Catholic population of America would be joined with enthusiasm and devotion by millions of the adherents to other religions, and by those who have no religious affiliation or interest, but who are believers in human freedom, particularly as found in the United States of America.

It would probably take something like a successful revolution or civil war to establish such a system. Such a nightmare seems wholly impossible; certainly the current advocates of universal public schools would be almost unanimously opposed to the use of force. Catholic education, therefore, will never be given up in America in any of its aspects except at the decision of Catholics themselves.

Anyone who has been interested in the controversies in the field of education in recent years must know that speeches, articles, and books in opposition to religious schools, especially Catholic parochial schools, are quite common. I have read, listened to, and participated in, a number of discussions of this type. But I have never known of a hostile criticism of parochial schools concerning the alleged inadequacies of faults in the actual operation of these schools that was an informed discussion. Their opponents regularly present arguments against the existence of the parochial schools, almost without exception based on erroneous assumptions with not even an attempt to prove the unfavorable implications or explicit charges covered by the assumptions. An outstanding example is the recent book by Dr. James Bryant Conant, *Education and Liberty*,[1] and his speech, "Education the Engine of Democracy," given before the American Association of School Administrators in Boston, April 7, 1952.[2]

Dr. Conant, for many years president of Harvard University, is probably the most influential opponent of religious and other private education in America; and at the same time he spoke and wrote his book he was still president of one of the most powerful, and in my opinion, one of the best private educational institutions, not only in America, but in the world. Interestingly, his opposition to all but government-operated education stopped at the end of the high school level, so his particular area of the college and university levels were not included in his indictment.

The basic false assumptions on which Dr. Conant rested his whole attack were expressed *first* in his statement that religious education is "endangering the American principle of a single public school system for all youth." There is obviously no such American principle, and there never has been; this is only the uni-

---

[1] (Cambridge: Harvard University Press, 1953.)
[2] *The Saturday Review* (New York), May 3, 1952.

versal principle of totalitarian dictatorships. It can be found no where in the world out of the reach of the guns of such tyrannies. His *second* fundamental assumption was: "The greater the proportion of our youth who fail to attend our public schools and who receive their education elsewhere, the greater the threat to our democratic unity." Uniformity, a thoroughly un-American concept, not the unity in diversity which is implied in the American idea of the "right to be different," would almost inevitably be the result of Dr. Conant's program.

The Conant speech and the book which followed it were severely criticized by both clergy and laity, both Catholic and Protestant, and school men in both religious and nonreligious schools. The Very Reverend James A. Pike, dean of the Episcopal Cathedral of St. John the Divine, New York, remarked that Dr. Conant, as the president of a private university, was "really sawing off the limb on which he sits." [3]

[3] *New York Times,* April 12, 1952. For extended criticism of the Conant documents, see articles by Archbishop Richard J. Cushing of Boston and Allan V. Heeley, headmaster of the Lawrenceville School, both in the issue of *The Saturday Review* mentioned above. Also a long article by J. M. O'Neill, "Education and Liberty," *Social Order* (St. Louis), Summer, 1953, reprinted in *The Catholic Mind* (New York), January 17, 1954, and a shorter discussion, "Religious Education and American Democracy," *Vital Speeches of the Day* (New York), May 15, 1952, a speech at the opening of the annual convention of the National Catholic Educational Association, Kansas City, Missouri, April 15, 1952.

It is regrettable that some people, or more specifically, a number of writers and speakers, are so devoted
to secular education that they are satisfied to remain
almost totally uninformed concerning Catholic education. It seems highly probable that adequate understanding of what religious education does for the people of the United States would gain the approval of
the religious schools by most of their present opponents
who actually believe in our American freedoms, particularly freedom of religion, opinion, press, speech, and
education. If religious and private education disap-
pears from the American scene to give place to public
education only, that will provide the perfect and universal foundation for the introduction (or perpetuation, once it is introduced) of totalitarian dictatorship
by either a single dictator or a majority political group.
The suppression of religious schools in favor of only
government-directed schools is the first requisite of
totalitarianism as has been widely demonstrated in the
last few decades.

In the United States of America, obviously, the majority of the people will have to become quite totalitarian minded, devoted to dictatorship, and willing to
have our freedoms disappear before we can have universal public education, because universal public education in this country can never come except by force.
It is inconceivable that the religious people of this

country—Protestant, Catholic, and Jewish—will ever voluntarily give up religious education.

There is one other theoretical possibility if two policies should be pursued together: first, that public funds in tremendous amounts will be given to public schools and colleges, enabling them to pay fantastic salaries to teachers and administrators and to have magnificent buildings, laboratories, libraries, and equipment; and second, that public assistance of any kind will be denied to any educational institution which is not a public institution and under government control. Such a double program might starve out the religious education institutions by making competition impossible. I have no fear that this will actually happen because I have too much confidence in America's devotion to human freedom. However, it is a possibility that should be held in mind in considering many questions that are coming up in the near future, such as federal aid to education, the interference with state and local control of public education (as by the Supreme Court in the McCollum case [4]) and attempts to discriminate against racial or religious groups. I like Dr. Rommen's statement: "The true danger to liberty is a ministry of public and popular enlightenment with too complete a control over education. The mere existence of free schools of the Church has done

[4] 333 U.S. 203 (1948), *op. cit.*

more to protect the liberty of education than all the oratory of freedom." [5]

In an earlier book,[6] I noted the similarities between the small Protestant colleges and the small Catholic colleges. During twenty-two years on the faculty of the University of Wisconsin and the University of Michigan, I became very well acquainted with many small Protestant colleges of the Middle West. I came to know their circumstances and the conditions surrounding their students very well. Most of these colleges have the same financial problems that most small Catholic colleges have. They need more teachers, higher salaries, more and better buildings, laboratories and libraries, and all of the other helps to education which only money can buy. But on the other hand they have many of the helps to the best education which money cannot buy. The men and women on their faculties seem to be there through essentially the same motivations that cause Catholic young men to enter the priesthood and Catholic young women to enter the teaching sisterhoods. They are trying, in addition to teaching "regular" subjects, to promote religion, morality, and idealism in their students and, in my opinion, most of them are doing a fine job. I have known many of their

[5] Heinrich Rommen, *The State and Catholic Thought* (St. Louis: D. Herter Book Co., 1947), p. 361.

[6] J. M. O'Neill, *Catholicism and American Freedom* (New York: Harper & Bros., 1949), pp. 102–104.

graduates well. I have had them as students in the graduate schools at Wisconsin, Michigan, and Northwestern universities. My opinion, as a Catholic who has had nearly half a century in teaching in various parts of the United States, is that the elimination of the small Protestant denominational colleges would be a calamity. It should please no informed American who believes in human freedom and democracy, regardless of his attitude toward positive religion. It goes without saying, I trust, that I have the same opinion of the result of the elimination of the small Catholic colleges.

It is my impression, though I cannot substantiate it by quoting figures, that the Catholic educational institutions in this country are, on the whole, stronger than the comparable Protestant institutions of the same rank; stronger because I believe they are, on the whole, larger in faculty and in student body and, therefore, have a larger proportion of potential backers devoted to them and also because American Catholics are accustomed to providing more money for education than any other religious group in America. They probably could resist more effectively, and therefore survive longer under, any governmental attempt to eliminate them by force, or to so support public education as to wean practically all the public away from them in favor of the government-controlled educational institutions.

So I believe that any largely successful movement to eliminate religious education in our country would probably result in eliminating many Protestant institutions but would leave standing a considerable number of Catholic ones.

This does not mean that at the present time Catholic education is perfect, or near perfect, throughout the United States.

Monsignor William E. McManus, assistant director of the Education Department of the National Catholic Welfare Council,[7] clearly does not so consider it. He recognizes the weaknesses that are resulting from what he calls "a 'seller's market' with a huge, record breaking backlog of unfilled orders for Catholic education." He estimates that by "1966 or 1967 our nationwide high school enrollment should also be doubled. These predictions are made on the assumption that in the future our elementary schools will continue to enroll three of every five Catholic grade school age children, and that our high schools will enroll about three of every ten Catholic adolescents. For the indefinite future, the ideal of having every Catholic child in a Catholic school seems utterly unattainable, and we might as well stop dreaming about it." He reports: "Double the amount of facilities will be needed to maintain the present ratio of Catholics in Catholic

[7] *The Catholic Mind* (New York), December, 1954, pp. 710–17.

and non-Catholic schools." Monsignor McManus strongly supports doing everything possible to overcome the two principal handicaps which hinder parochial schools today—lack of sufficient staff and sufficient buildings. Both are obstacles to the best education and both can be properly and completely cured only by money. He says:

Recruit competent lay teachers, give them status as full-fledged members of the faculty; guarantee them security and tenure; pay them a living wage. One of every ten teachers in our elementary schools today is a lay person. Within ten years, I think, one of every five will be a lay person if our schools are expanded to accommodate anticipated increases in enrollment. No longer may the lay teacher be regarded as a "substitute for a sick Sister"; the lay teacher now is an indispensable member of Catholic school faculties and is entitled to the respect and confidence of parents, the laity in general and the clergy.

Maintain high professional standards. Every Catholic school pupil has a strict right in justice to a program of studies which in essentials is in no way inferior to the program of public schools. That is the official teaching of the Council of Baltimore. Crowding fifty, sixty and seventy pupils into a classroom may seem like zeal for Catholic education, but in many cases, it actually is a serious violation of the pupils' right to satisfactory and efficient education. Subjecting children to partially trained teachers is an injustice to both pupils and the teachers. The laudable ambition to enroll all applicants should never be perverted into an excuse for lowering professional school standards.

We are reaching the point, ladies and gentlemen, where we will have to hang out "no more room" signs. There are many parishes throughout the United States that in the future will have to turn children away. The practice in some places of overcrowding classrooms is going to boomerang on the whole system. State school authorities already are watching what we are doing in this regard.

Develop a reasonable procedure to select the students to be admitted to available accommodations. This is probably going to be the toughest problem of the future. In my opinion, accepting students on a first-come, first-served basis is not a reasonable procedure.

One of the recommendations of Monsignor McManus that is directly in line with the chief purpose of this book concerns more help to Catholic students in public schools:

Utilize the Catholic schools to provide systematic religious instruction and extracurricular activities for Catholic public school pupils. This is a most important point. Every Catholic child of school age has a right to a reasonably convenient opportunity for systematic religious instruction from a competent teacher. Catholic education authorities are obliged to provide this opportunity. This obligation to give the minimum of religious instruction to all has a priority over the duty to give the fullness of Catholic education to as many as can be enrolled in Catholic schools. Catholic public school pupils, therefore, should have first claim upon Catholic school facilities during after-school hours and on holidays. . . . No Catholic school faculty may say its work is done when it has cared for only its student body. Saving the elect is relatively easy; saving the lost sheep is much harder, but it is no less a duty upon all engaged in Catholic school work.

Every parish school ought to have a home and school association. It is most important that the parents of the school children, the pastors, the school principals and the teachers of the school come together for frank and constructive consideration of their work in education and of the needs of our schools in the future. The Catholic school enterprise is not a mere business in which the Catholic Church renders a service to the people. On the contrary, the Catholic school enterprise is a cooperative venture in which the Church, the Bishops, the pastors, the school principals and the parents have a joint interest. It only makes common sense that they pool their energies and their thoughts to develop reasonable plans for the future of our schools.[7]

In addition to the contribution of religious education to the religious faith, moral training, and the personal happiness which flows from these to millions of Americans, I believe that the religious schools of this country are a first necessity if we are to preserve our American freedoms. There is no valid evidence in human history that our freedoms could long survive universal public education exclusively government directed.

It seems obvious that all active Catholics, regardless of the degree of their acquaintance with secular education, and especially without regard to their opinion as to its merits or demerits, should be concerned over the absence of religious guidance and religious service to the many of the millions of Catholic students who are, and who must be in the foreseeable future, in secular educational institutions. No great enthusiast for secular education and no opponent of religious education need be concerned about recruiting Catholic students for secular institutions. Apparently, millions of them for some time to come will have to go to secular institutions if they get formal education. An important problem for Catholic America is, therefore, what can be done to help *as much as possible*, not simply the minority of Catholic students in Catholic educational institutions, but also the majority who are in the secular institutions. These are the majority of the future Catholics of America.

These are some items in a program of action that would do much to make the foreseeable future more satisfactory to every shade of Catholic opinion. One is a general awareness of what the conditions actually are in secular education—its dangers and its possibilities for good. This problem is discussed more at length in succeeding chapters.

Catholic students are going to be in the secular colleges. What are we going to do for them? First, we should prepare them realistically for meeting the real conditions which they will have to meet. I have rarely known a Catholic much experienced in secular education who considered the dangers to religion and morals and patriotism as very great *for a Catholic who is well prepared when he enters a secular college.* Such preparation is not furthered by sweeping denunciations of all secular education or simply taking the position that Catholics should keep out of it. But only good can result from preparing them much better than many of them have been prepared in a knowledge of Catholicism and in how to take part in polite and enlightened discussion to correct errors which come up in their presence.

The problems of improving and extending the facilities of Catholic education are tremendous. The Denver *Register* [8] carried a front-page story with large headlines proclaiming that 42,750 more teachers will be needed in Catholic elementary and high schools by 1965; 2,723 new high schools, and 1,927 new elementary schools will have to be built by 1965 at a cost of $479,000,000.

The present teaching staff was given as 96,371 (religious, 89,487; lay, 6,884) in elementary schools, and 25,360 in high schools. This story was based on the

[8] August 21, 1955.

recent survey by the Mathematics Department of Manhattan College.

The Catholic press recently has contained many statements to the effect that the Catholic schools must somehow raise the salaries of the lay teachers if they are to have a competent professional staff. The average annual salary of lay teachers in Catholic colleges and universities (which was probably higher than the average salary of lay teachers in elementary and high schools) was in 1950 approximately $3,000 a year.[9]

To get a full staff of teachers to provide Catholic education for the *same proportion* of Catholic students now in these institutions (about 50 per cent in the elementary schools and 30 per cent in the high schools), the number of lay teachers will have to be greatly increased. Just how much extra money this will take is impossible to estimate at all accurately on any figures now available.

For the increased lay faculty on the college and university level, the expenditure would probably go far beyond the additional $30,000,000 per year estimated as necessary to raise the average annual salary to $5,000.[10] At the present time while exact figures are not now available, in the the city of New York there are probably not more than 50,000 students registered in

[9] A. Kargan, "Financial Problems of Catholic Colleges," *America* (New York), April 11, 1953.
[10] *Ibid.*

Catholic colleges and universities and some 200,000 registered in public and private non-Catholic colleges and universities. In the four New York City municipal colleges the current registration is 78,699. How many of these are Catholics cannot be accurately reported, but the best estimates indicate that the number is about equal to the number in the Catholic institutions, most of which have some non-Catholic students.

The salary scale for lay teachers in Catholic colleges and universities has been rising in recent years, and figures of even a few years ago cannot be taken as the salaries of 1955–1956 and after. The salaries paid in private colleges and universities, whether religious or secular, are not public documents, and in some institutions are closely guarded secrets known only to administrative officers. I know that there are private secular colleges in which the salaries paid to members of a department are not known even to the chairmen of the departments. Public salary scales are, of course, public documents. On the basis of cordial cooperation of the few Catholic institutions to which I sent inquiries, I learned that in these typical colleges and universities of various types, full professors' salaries ranged from $6200 to $8500, and beginning salaries for instructors, from $3400 to $3800. In the four public colleges of New York City the salaries prescribed by the state law are: professors $8700 to $12,450; associate professors $6900 to $9850; assistant professors, $5508 to $8450; instructors $4860 to $7350. All have mandatory annual increments.

If the standards recommended by Monsignor McManus of the National Catholic Welfare Council are introduced and maintained, the sum of money needed in the foreseeable future by Catholic educational institutions to cover operating expenses for the equivalent of the buildings and the personnel of the present, plus salary increases, staff increases, and new buildings, will be a gigantic sum. The amount is, of course, impossible to set down with any definiteness, but probably when it is added up accurately in the end, it will have to be expressed in millions—if not in billions—of dollars.

In discussing the general situation in religious education, it must be kept in mind that there are many types of religious schools outside the Catholic system. We have full-time day schools under various religious auspices in the United States, in addition to the Catholic ones. Some of the many schools under private auspices are connected with religious bodies, and some are not. According to a story in the Denver *Register* [11], the United States Department of Commerce and Labor reports that private school building (of all kinds) during the year 1954 cost $560,000,000 an in-

[11] January 15, 1955.

crease of 31 per cent over 1953. In the same year, public school construction cost $2,065,000,000, an increase of only 20 per cent over the previous year. In other words, private school construction in that year was increasing much more rapidly than public school construction.

Any belief that the Catholic population of school and college age is going to remain substantially level or decrease in the near future seems wholly unrealistic. Monsignor William E. McManus, of the Education Department of the National Catholic Welfare Council,[12] gave some interesting statistics on infant baptisms. Here is the table:

1944	710,648
1946	738,314
1948	937,314
1950	973,544
1952	1,077,184
1953	1,094,872

One of every four children born in the United States last year, according to Monsignor McManus, was baptized a Catholic and he mentions the probability of another "baby boom" resulting from marriages in the 1940's that may raise the infant baptism rate as high as 1,400,000 per year. In Connecticut, almost 61 per cent of the babies born in 1954 were baptized in the Catholic Church, an increase of 45,469 for the year,

[12] *Op. cit.*

bringing the year's total to 1,161,304. The increase in 1953 over the total for 1952 was 38,651.[13]

Monsignor McManus estimated that at the end of the coming decade, the high school enrollment of the nation should also be doubled, and he concluded this part of his discussion with the remark that a Catholic education for every Catholic child "seems utterly unobtainable."

Of course, there are weaknesses in the physical plants of the educational systems in the United States at the present time. The growth has been too rapid for new construction and repair to keep up with the demand, either in public or private education, and Catholic educational authorities, as well as public educational authorities, are well aware of the fact that overcrowding in schoolrooms is a severe interference with the proper education of the children; it is also a serious handicap to getting and keeping an adequate teaching staff.

Surveys and estimates differ somewhat but they all seem to indicate roughly the same sort of increases needed in the next decade. Dr. Urban H. Fleege, of the National Catholic Education Association,[14] wrote: "Conservative estimates call for the building of at least 43,000 additional classrooms and the recruiting of

---

[13] *The Catholic Transcript* (Hartford), May 26, 1955.
[14] *The Tablet* (Brooklyn, N.Y.), June 5, 1954.

60,000 additional teachers by 1960, if we are to continue to provide Catholic educational facilities for but half of our Catholic children. After 1960, classroom and teacher needs will increase yearly even beyond what the annual need will be between now and 1960. . . . Today 46% of Catholic elementary school children are attending a Catholic school. If Catholics are to continue providing a Catholic education for even less than half of all their children of this age, they will have to build and equip 30,500 new elementary schools between now and 1960–61. This building program is estimated at present school construction costs at close to $1,000,000,000. For financing this needed expansion program during the next 7 years, Catholics will have to recruit, educate and have ready to step in the classroom over 27,000 additional elementary school teachers, not counting replacements needed due to retirement and death among teacher personnel." Again, "Catholics are not confronted with a mere emergency situation. The problem is not only here to stay but will reappear each year beyond 1960 with increasing severity." Dr. Fleege adds an interesting remark outside of the estimates of the difficulties in financial and personnel matters of the Catholic educational institutions in the next decade. He says: "Every school day, Catholics of the United States are saving the taxpayers over $4,000,000 in maintenance and operating costs alone, not counting the huge sums involved in capital outlay."

As shown in the last chapter, the figures available at the present time from recent surveys indicate that there were, in the year 1954–1955, a total of 5,226,707 Catholic children and youth getting their formal education in non-Catholic institutions. There seems to be no reasonable basis for assuming that this figure will not greatly increase in the foreseeable future.

The problem of the distribution of Catholic students between non-Catholic and Catholic institutions, and the concomitant problem of how the Church is to attend to the religious needs of the millions in the non-Catholic educational institutions, has been much discussed in the Catholic press in recent months. So far, I have seen no figures for a carefully based estimate of exactly what the grand total of Catholic students in non-Catholic educational institutions will amount to at the close of the next decade, but it seems fair to assume that it will be in the neighborhood of at least 6,000,000 and this brings us around again to the precise problem of this book—what can or should be done in attempting to serve the religious needs of between 5,000,000 and 6,000,000 Catholics in secular education. Admittedly, this problem of the religious needs of these young Catholics is a complicated one. Admittedly there are some dangers, as there are in other possible conditions of life for American youth. Some Catholics abandon their religion while attending non-Catholic institutions. I know of no figures that show to what extent this is true. We also know that a good many non-Catholic students attending non-Catholic institutions become converts to the Catholic Church. But the problem of how to meet anti-Catholicism, agnosticism, atheism, and secularism in secular institutions for the Catholic student is unquestionably one that American Catholics should seriously consider. And it should be discussed by the counselors, advisors, parents, and teachers of the students *before* they go away to college.

Perhaps the one consideration that is universally applicable to this problem is that in each instance of its appearance it is likely to have some features not found in other instances, i.e., the magnitude of the problem varies from college to college, department to department, course to course, instructor to instructor, and student to student. Each instance is an individual human problem and should be treated as such. There seems to be an unnecessarily wide divergence of opinion among American Catholics as to the danger that faces a Catholic student in a non-Catholic institution. Some seem to think that there is no danger at all for the particular students whom they know best, and especially for those for whom they have specific responsibility; some have actually said that they would rather see their children dead than in a public high school. Both of these extreme positions are unrealistic, and must rest on an almost total lack of knowledge of secular education in America. Both are quite different from any opinion I have ever heard expressed by Catholics who were intimately acquainted with non-Catholic education.

3

Anti-Catholicism in Secular Education

Contrary to the belief of some Catholics, there is, in my opinion, very little anti-Catholic bigotry at the present time in secular education in America; but there is a tremendous amount of misinformation and misunderstanding among the students and teachers in all types of secular educational institutions. The same thing is doubtless true among journalists, government official and employees, non-Catholic clergyman, and other religious workers. Many men of good will are so uninformed and have heard untruths about Catholics and Catholicism repeated so often that they easily accept the shocking "scholarship" of those who are selling volumes of misinformation as valid reporting and criticism, since it is usually dressed up in spurious footnotes that present the external appearance of sound research.

I have been told that in some schools, colleges, and universities these books are actually recommended to students as dependable sources of information on

Catholicism. While I do not know of any provable instances of this, I have no doubt that it is true. But I doubt if it is often true that this is done by teachers who know the almost total unreliability of these volumes. These teachers probably have been innocently misled by other equally uninformed (or possibly bigoted or dishonest) reviewers of the books of those who are making money by falsely attacking the Catholic Church and their American Catholic fellow citizens as enemies of American freedom and democracy.

I have never known, in any of the faculties of which I have been a member, anyone whom I could recognize and identify as aggressively anti-Catholic, either ignorantly or knowingly. I have never known an instance of a teacher or an official in one of these institutions whom I could honestly label as a bigot. I have known none who seemed to have as a purpose the spreading of misinformation about the Catholic Church or American Catholics. In other words, I have known of no one in the administration or teaching staffs of these institutions whom I could conscientiously put in the class of Paul Blanshard,[1] James Hastings Nichols,[2] of the School of Theology, University of Chicago, and George W. Elderkin,[3] Professor

[1] *American Freedom and Catholic Power* (Boston: Beacon Press, 1949).

[2] *Democracy in the Churches* (Philadelphia: The Westminster Press, 1951).

[3] *The Roman Catholic Problem* (New York: Vantage Press, 1954).

Emeritus, Princeton University. Substantiating data on the Blanshard and Nichols books are easily available.[4] The Elderkin book is almost wholly a superficial sweeping up of the chief misrepresentations and insults of his unscholarly predecessors in the business of anti-Catholic propaganda.

I have never been a member of the faculties of the University of Chicago nor of Princeton University, and I have no direct knowledge as to what extent Professors Nichols and Elderkin attempted to spread their strange ideas of Catholicism on the campuses of these great universities. However, from what I know of the faculties of these institutions, and particularly of some of the distinguished Catholic laymen who hold important positions in them, I should be much surprised to learn that Professors Nichols and Elderkin were very active or effective in anti-Catholic campaigns in these universities.

No informed person will deny that there are in secular education many faculty members and students who are nonreligious, and antireligious at some times and to some extent. They have no personal commitment to any religion, and, if occasion arises for them to be either pro or anti religion, will doubtless be anti. They are almost always antireligion when they take a

---

[4] O'Neill, *Catholicism and American Freedom,* and "Scholarship and Emotional Voltage," *Thought* (New York), Winter, 1951–52.

stand rather than anti-Catholic. However, it is probably true that their sharpest antireligion remarks will be phrased in anti-Catholic terms—for which there will be many contributing factors and different explanations. Probably the majority of these potential antireligion individuals are neither well enough informed nor sufficiently interested in religion to think about it or to talk about it. Religion probably bores most people who know little or nothing about it. However, the uninformed people who do much talking and writing about religion are apparently those who are busy making money out of their ignorance as a cherished financial asset. They can probably do a smoother job by carefully avoiding information than they could by getting the facts and then lying about them. This type of publicist is naturally not often found on the faculties of educational institutions.

However, most of the potentially antireligion people on college faculties have apparently left Protestantism, or become uninterested in it; but they still know something about it, and are somewhat sympathetic toward it. They know very little about the Catholic Church or the beliefs, practices, and aspirations of American Catholics. So their smoldering antireligion feelings, when they break out, are likely to break out as more anti-Catholic than anti-Protestant. It seems highly improbable that any well-informed Catholic student can be endangered by the remarks of such people; the ill-informed young Catholic will be in danger wherever he is.

A priest, writing under the pen name of Ralph H. Strode, discussed at some length the danger to the faith of Catholic students in non-Catholic colleges. He lists six phases of this danger: *The Scholarly Approach* (not against any religion, uses Catholic scholars in his work, friends in all faiths—but *as a scholar* he asks his students to leave their religon at the door with their overshoes); *Ridicule and Sarcasm*; *The Big Word Technique*; *The Daily Grapeshot* (a campaign of attrition, each remark insignificant, but the cumulative effect important) *The Faculty Coffee* (the Catholic student swept away by being—apparently for the first time in his life—in a home of a "cultured, gracious family.") [5]

I am of the opinion that most Catholics who have much acquaintance with non-Catholic colleagues in secular colleges, and have known hundreds of Catholic students in these colleges, will agree that Father Strode's concept of the Catholic student is that of an unusually simple-minded fellow, inexcusably ignorant of Catholic doctrine and practice, and seemingly unaware that there are any cultured, gracious *Catholic*

[5] "Subversion of Faith by Intellectuals," *America* (New York), October 9, 1954.

homes. It would appear that the Catholic student who would succumb to the sort of dangers to his faith depicted here must necessarily have had little or no intelligent preparation for going to any college. He would probably have dropped away from the Church between the ages of eighteen and thirty regardless of where he was or what he was doing—unless at about the age of eighteen he married a Catholic girl who was much better trained in her religion than he was.

This is not to deny that there are dangers in non-Catholic colleges, especially for the badly prepared student, and particularly in colleges which do not have: (a) a Catholic priest assigned to attend to the religious needs of the Catholic students, and (b) some Catholic faculty members who are good enough in their respective fields to win and hold the respect of their colleagues, and well enough acquainted with Catholic doctrine and history to be able to answer (or to find the answer) to questions from colleagues and students. In such a college the Father Strode types of attack on Catholicism will be practically nonexistent, and the surrender to them will be found only among the dull or hopelessly uninformed Catholic students who have received no specific preparation to enable them to get the good and avoid the bad in secular education.

Unquestionably, some Catholic students drop out

of the Church while in attendance at a non-Catholic college or shortly thereafter—some of them for reasons that have nothing to do with anything that happened in the college or for which their experience *as students* was in any way responsible. Also, some young people cease to be Catholics who never go to college at all or even go to Catholic colleges. The dangers to Catholic youth everywhere should be accurately understood and discussed and, so far as possible, guarded against. However, it seems possible, as Father James J. Maguire wrote, that Father Strode's article "may possibly serve to deter a very few parents from sending their children to secular colleges.[6] It will more probably serve to alienate the many men of good will who are beginning to look to the Church with new respect. If unchallenged and widely read, its most certain effect would be to make Catholics appear slightly ridiculous." My only amendment to this statement would be to change "slightly" to "thoroughly." I have never known a Catholic who was intimately acquainted with secular college education to express an opinion in agreement with Father Strode; I am confident that almost unanimously they would agree with Father Maguire that "a nationwide campaign designed to emphasize the corrosiveness of secular education might, if buttressed by canon-

[6] "Another Look at Subversion of Faith," *America* (New York), December 4, 1954.

ical legislation, have some temporary effect. But its total adverse effect on the Church would beggar description. . . . It would also create in the Church a new and most disastrous type of ghetto mentality."

Father Maguire was clearly not trying to persuade more students to go to secular colleges instead of to Catholic colleges. He was trying to spread information which seems to me wholly correct in regard to the actual situation in the matter of danger to faith in secular colleges and universities.

He reports that, actually, really effective atheists or agnostics are considerably more rare than effective religious teachers. I agree with his report and believe that most Catholics experienced in non-Catholic higher education will do the same. In addition to the formal teachers of religion, of which I had a few as colleagues, there were many more men and women of considerable religious influence than there were those who could be recognized as active atheists or agnostics, though there were a few of these. Probably the majority of the faculties of which I was a member were essentially indifferent to religion. Doubtless many of them were formally listed in some religious organization or another, but apparently "they didn't work at it." Some were very active and sincere members of Protestant or Jewish religious organizations.

In regard to the trouble spots in the curriculum, so

far as our present topic is concerned, Father Strode
mentions sociology and its related disciplines and the
philosophy of education. I should say that unquestionably sociology and philosophy are the two departments
in which one is most likely to find definitely agnostic
or atheistic teachers, and teachers who are inexcusably
uninformed on some of the religious topics which they
discuss in the classroom. They would be "sitting ducks"
for any well-informed sophomore. However, it would
be a mistake to think that every such teacher is actively anti-Catholic in the classroom or out of it, or trying to change the religious faith of his students. It is
true that there is some compelling evidence, which has
necessarily come to my attention, which shows that in
the departments of sociology, philosophy, and education there can be found some professors who are clearly
anti-Catholic in regard to certain matters in education
and religion. Whether this attitude is based on inno-
cent ignorance or deliberate dishonesty is doubtless
known only to these professors. Such evidence is to be
found in abundance in reviews by professors in these
departments of two books already mentioned, Paul
Blanshard's *American Freedom and Catholic Power,*
and my answering volume, *Catholicism and American
Freedom.*

I agree with Father Maguire that in the natural sciences generally there is little place for the personal

philosophy of the instructor and very little reporting of any antireligious views from the teachers in science departments. I have known a few teachers in these fields who described themselves as atheists, but I never heard even a hint that they were antireligious or anti-Catholic in their teaching or *in their social attitudes.* I knew one who so labeled himself who was greatly disappointed because he couldn't get his son into a Catholic parochial school in New York City. When I asked him why he wanted this, he answered, "It's the best damned school in the city!"

Based on his many years as a Newman Club director, Father Maguire concludes that " all this adds up to the conclusion that the day of smug agnosticism is past. It still lingers in educational and sociological circles, but the day of its dominance is over."

However, the day of trying to dominate American education through the use of innuendo by those who have no evidence is not over. This is demonstrated by the recent little volume *Public Education and the Future of America.*[7] The basic assumptions of this booklet seem to be, first, that public schools *only* have made a variety of significant contributions to the American way of life; and, *second,* that democracy, and

[7] Published by the Educational Policies Commission of the National Education Association and the American Association of School Administrators, 1201 Sixteenth Street, Washington, D.C.

other highly desirable features of American life, will survive and be properly expanded *only* if public education becomes universal. These positions necessarily are not explicitly stated and accompanied by supporting evidence—none being available.

I think it probable that most of the specific claims made in this book for public education are true, but also that most of these claims are equally true in regard to private and religious education in America. Doubtless all American schools, public and private, religious and secular, contribute to most of the things that the Educational Policies Committee attributes on page after page only to public education.

This book reports that the American leaders in education in the latter years of the eighteenth century, in planning for the future, thought that schools (unqualified, which must mean all schools) should be "controlled by civil government." (p. 12.) No evidence whatever is offered in support of this statement, probably because no such evidence can be found. Clearly no such plan has ever received wide acceptance in America. Certainly it has never been approved by any Congress of the United States, general convention, referendum, or any other instrument for the expression of the opinion of the American people. Only one state has ever demonstrated a belief in universal public education: Oregon in 1922 passed a law requiring all children to attend public schools. In 1925 the Supreme Court of the United States in an unanimous opinion [8] declared the Oregon statute unconstitutional.

There follows (p. 13) an equally strange statement that "by the middle of the nineteenth century a system of universal public education with its roots in the prophetic ideas of the 1790's was well on its way toward realization." Again, the authors present no evidence that by around 1850 (or at any other time in our history) *universal* public education was well on its way to adoption. They did present some pages of discussion of certain forces which indicated the well-known desire for more and better education among substantially all groups in America in that period. If there had been any evidence that a system of universal public education was greatly in demand, these forces might possibly have been cited as part of the explanation of such a demand. However, this statement as given is one of the most fantastic in this strange volume.

The period mentioned, "by the middle of the nineteenth century," must mean before 1850. This was the exact period of the most intense religious strife in the history of American education. The public schools of the time were essentially Trinitarian Protestant schools

[8] Pierce v. Society of Sisters, 268 U.S. 510.

run at public expense (rather naturally, of course, considering the cultural background, both in Europe and America, of most of the Americans of that day). This was the time of the bitter contests brought about by the complete public support of Protestant schools and the denial of any public assistance to Catholic schools; of the flogging or suspension of Catholic pupils in public schools for refusing to participate in Protestant worship and study; of the burning of the Ursuline Convent in Boston in 1835; and of the frightful Philadelphia riots of 1844. In these riots two Catholic churches and one seminary were burned, thirteen persons killed and fifty wounded, because the Philadelphia Board of Education granted the request of the Catholic Bishop of Philadelphia that Catholic pupils in public schools be allowed to use the Douay version of the Bible in the Compulsory Bible study and be excused from Protestant worship. I recommend a bit of reading in American social history in the works of eminent non-Catholic historians.[9]

Today there seems to be a substantially unanimous opinion among Americans of all classes, types, and creeds that the individual states properly make certain

[9] For instance, Howard K. Beale, of the University of North Carolina, *A History of Freedom of Teaching in American Schools* (New York: Scribner's, 1941); Ray Allen Billington, of Northwestern University, *The Protestant Crusade* (New York: Macmillan, 1938; reissued New York: Rinehart & Co., 1952); Merle Curti, of the University of Wisconsin, *The Social Ideas of American Educators* (New York: Scribner's, 1935).

basic requirements in education, but this is very far from the belief that there should be no school system except that conducted by the state to provide the fundamental education for the whole people. A public school system to which all students would be admitted if their parents wished them to go there, but which no one would be compelled to attend if he attended some other school recognized by the state educational authorities, is, I believe, universally approved. The voluntary use of the public system of education by those who wish to use it is fine; the compulsory use of it would end American religious and educational freedom. If, as claimed (p. 20), it has been "found that the broad elements from the various creeds on which all agreed could be taught in school, leaving doctrinal education to the home and church," it is most unfortunate that the authors of this booklet did not report what the broad elements of the various creeds on which all agreed actually are.

Concerning the constant praise of the way in which the public schools have served all segments of the population, the authors seem not to have known, or to have omitted to mention, the fact that the public educational system of America for some decades was essentially a system of Protestant schools at public expense, and that Protestant religious observances were a regular part of the activities of most public school

systems until about 1900. Also, when they mentioned
(p. 21) that "one of the most characteristic features of
the American public school system, *local control by
local boards of education*,[10] legally responsible to the
state," they again either did not know, or preferred not
to mention, the famous McCollum decision of the
United States Supreme Court in 1948. In this decision
the Supreme Court took out of the hands of "local
boards of education legally responsible to the State"
the control of education in Champaign, Illinois. In so
doing the Court invalidated the laws passed by the
state legislature, the procedures approved by the State
Department of Education, and the decision of the Supreme Court of the State of Illinois, in order to dictate
that the Board of Education of Champaign, Illinois,
could not permit, in school hours, the use of classrooms that were not otherwise used, by pupils who
were not at that hour assigned to any other duties in
the school, to carry on an activity approved by the
Board of Education and by a large number of parents
in various religious denominations in the community—
but which was opposed by the parents of one child.
This was the contribution of the United States Supreme
Court in that case to the operation of democracy in the
control of local problems, to religious and educational
freedom, and to the responsibility of state educational

[10] Italics supplied.

authorities in cooperation with the local Board of Education.[11]

The authors (p. 36) write: "as Society placed on the common school the responsibility for educating all its children." This is, of course, something that American society has never done, and which it is not likely to do so long as the principles of the state and federal bills of rights remain alive in this country.

The authors remark (p. 86): "The future would be jeopardized . . . if any sizeable part of the population grew up possessed of alien outlooks and habits." This seems true—and trite—but irrelevant to any realistic discussion of American education. In the general atmosphere of this book, this remark is in thoroughly bad taste. If the authors believe that there exists any threat that any part of the educational machinery in this country is producing a population of American citizens "of alien outlooks and habits"—other than the Communist infiltration of some parts of the *public school system* which have been exposed and presumably been taken care of—they should specify the parts or places in which this sort of thing is being done, and, with the assistance of substantially all intelligent and responsible Americans, put a stop to it.

If any schools or levels of education, in any sections of the country, were proved to be guilty of such prac-

[11] For further details see pp. 108ff.

tices, I am confident that a remedy less drastic than "killing the patient to cure the disease," that is, by eliminating all the free schools, could be applied. The American people are not likely to become so panic-stricken as to adopt the universal and essential basis of all totalitarian dictatorships—total government control of education—in order to prevent the possible development of "alien outlooks and habits" in some people. If this were the appropriate remedy, some *public schools* would doubtless some time since have been suppressed in certain parts of the country where communist infiltration promoting "alien outlooks and habits" was rather marked.

Bishop Oxnam, in a forum discussion at the Harvard Law School, said: "I am opposed to the use of public funds for parochial education because under such a system public money can be spent to undermine the basic principles upon which the democratic order rests." Also, "Is a Jew to pay taxes for the support of Roman Catholic parochial education when he believes that in some quarters the emphasis is of such a nature as to contribute to anti-Semitism?" He was answered: "I suppose it is true that public funds could be spent in the parochial school system to develop subversive and antidemocratic and anti-Semitic ideas. They can also be spent—and have been spent—in public schools to accomplish exactly the same purpose. And anyone who has lived in public education as long as I have will not deny that statement." [12]

Of course, Jews pay taxes to support public schools in which anti-Semitism is practiced; the religious people of our country, of every group and denomination, pay taxes to support public schools in which agnosticism, atheism, materialism, and secularism not only may be promoted, but (with the blessing of the Supreme Court of the United States) are given a preferred position over positive religion; Christian Scientists pay taxes to support public schools in which physiology and bacteriology is taught, and to support public medical schools. And the plight of American Negroes in public education (to support which they pay taxes) is the outstanding disgrace to the freedom and equality expressed in our constitutions and believed in by probably the overwhelming majority of Americans. By the testimony to be found in various quarters, especially in the secular and Protestant press of the northern part of the country, the Catholic Church leads all other religious groups in trying to change this situation.

Until some of these evil influences are *proved* to be operative in some of the religious schools of the country, the insulting assumption that they are probably

[12] "Public Aid to Parochial Education," *Harvard Law School Forum* (Cambridge), March 16, 1951, pp. 29, 32, 44.

to be found in these schools should not be carelessly, or maliciously, circulated.

Remarks (pp. 86–87) concerning the unwritten laws and mores of American behavior and the service functions of public education, covering such topics as *honesty, personal cleanliness,* and *common courtesy,* suggest a rather narrow, insular, and unsophisticated view of America in contrast with the rest of the civilized world, and a thoroughly uninformed view of American private and religious education. This passage is not only in bad taste, but is inconsistent with the statement (p. 89) that "the needed school program must be intimately related to society—not a narrowly isolated or insulated form of education." This is an admirable quality in any program of education, but hardly one that is furthered by the present document.

The authors write (p. 91): "In the future with inevitable strains and tensions, the American people urgently need the vibrant strength that arises from voluntary unity." Excellent! Voluntary unity is fine and universally admired, but uniformity such as would come from an exclusively state-controlled system of education is its opposite and is completely contrary to American ideals, laws, principles, and traditions.

The authors are thoroughly correct in speaking (p. 92) of the American tradition which "emphasizes a voluntary unity that allows for diversity within the encompassing framework of common values. Such a unity, resting upon cultural pluralism seems to be endorsed on this particular page, but is essentially questioned on many other pages of this booklet.

On page 95, in commenting on the religious heterogeneity of this country, the authors say that Americans have "become singularly unified in allegiance to common moral and spiritual values" and then conclude that "the common schools have taught these values to the succeeding generations of Americans and through them have nurtured a moral unity within which a diversity of religious commitments has flourished." Most of the things mentioned on that page as moral and spiritual values would be accepted by all Americans. Most well-informed Americans would probably say that they rest almost totally on the religious teachings of the Judeo-Christian tradition. Any person who is well informed concerning the programs of the religious and private schools in America would agree that they, as well as the common schools, have taught these values to succeeding generations of Americans. Probably most people informed in regard to both public and religious schools would say that the latter had done this particular job better than it had been done by the public schools.

A Catholic administrator in a large secular institution writes:

It is my thought—shared by countless others, of course—that secularism is not a matter of teachers or courses of study, narrowly viewed. It is a state of mind, an accepted way of life. It comes about as a result of many factors, not the least important of which are educational influences in formal and informal ways. . . . The effectiveness of teaching and research in studies as they now exist are not under question here. Under question is the total view of the product—is he the whole man? If he is the cause is found outside the pattern of education as we find it in institutions not church related. This despite the fact that educational systems are blessed with countless men and women of religious convictions and high moral purpose. It rubs off on their students at times and its true influence can scarcely be measured. Does the irreligion of others rub off, too?

The best antidote for "catching" irreligion this way is the presence of some scholarly, competent Catholics on the faculty.

4

Catholics on Secular Faculties

I had a letter recently from a friend on the faculty of a large secular college whom I consider to be one of the best informed and most devoted Catholics of my acquaintance. He and his wife are about as *regular* Catholics as one could find. He wrote as follows:

"I have now completed fifteen years of full-time teaching in secular institutions. Seven of these years I was the only Catholic on the teaching staff and in two instances the first Catholic to join the faculty. I must say that I have never suffered any discrimination of any kind. Many of my colleagues had never before met a Catholic on equal social and educational terms, and I believe it was a revelation to some that a Catholic could be as intelligent and as well educated as themselves. But despite the surprise that my Catholicism elicited, I was always treated in a most friendly way." He touched upon one problem in Catholic education which only money will solve. "Frequently I am asked why I don't want to teach in a Catholic school." His answer was, "How am I to support my family? All the lay teachers in Catholic institutions with whom I am acquainted are either single or compelled to eke out their salaries by extra jobs."

He finds a disturbing "aspect of being a Catholic in secular education . . . is the lack of understanding and faint contempt that I sense on the part of some fellow Catholics who are engaged in less suspect occupations." He deplores "the deep conviction that our secular education is dangerous for the Catholic and they [some Catholics] can't see how anyone would be interested in devoting his life to it. The notion that there is a real need for Catholics in secular institutions strikes many Catholics of my acquaintance as naïve and absurd. They are, of course, not aware of the number of Catholics being educated in secular colleges and of the total impossibility of educating these numbers under existing conditions in Catholic schools."

The criticism and faint contempt, however, has had little effect on him. On the other side of the ledger, he refers to a former girl student who is "now a Carmelite nun, and five young men now studying for the priesthood in various seminaries who are all former members of our Newman Club." He gets particular satisfaction from the attitude of "two dear friends, one a priest (a Newman Club chaplain) and the other a nun (a Catholic college teacher), both of whom have encouraged me to stay in secular education—*as a leaven*," in the words of the priest.

Last year a Catholic layman mentioned a Catholic priest and two Catholic seminarians who were members of the student Catholic organization of which he had been director in recent years in the Protestant-related university in which he was a professor in the field of the social sciences. American Catholics should give a great deal of thought to the problem of promoting, in every legitimate way, the sound and acceptable preparation of personable, competent, and scholarly Catholics who will seek to enter the faculties of secular institutions.

Dr. Taylor, dean of the graduate school of Princeton University, has written:

"It ought to be recognized that, in the modern educational centres, outside the frankly confessional school and colleges, the growing menace of secularism, or even frank paganism, is most to be feared. We must, however, recognize that to the extent that we, convinced Christians, withdraw from the effort, to that extent we abandon the secular colleges to the secularists. Wherever the 'liberty of the act of faith' is conceded, whether in the university or the state, there devolves upon Catholics the duty to take their place in the organization and conduct of all affairs on the secular plane. Segregation in such circumstances might well become a sin of omission. Participation cannot be postponed until that ideal day, which, being ideal, must be recognized as remote and far from practical reality, when all men shall confess 'one faith, one baptism.' It is an unattainable ideal in the staffing of many Catholic colleges and universities. Why must we withdraw from centres where it cannot obtain?

"The Catholic intellectual placed in the neutralist environment of much of the modern educational society has to formulate a philosophy of life in such an environment. If he is a realist, he must recognize that he cannot wait for a religious unity which cannot be expected in any near future. He will recognize that while some may essay the advent of such a unity by a more and more penetrating analysis of religious concepts, the great majority must address themselves to the practical problems of adjustment to a pluralist society which undoubtedly will persist for a very long time."[1]

My experience, and the experience of many others who have spent decades in secular higher education, indicates that the answer to the problem is a larger number of properly qualified *Catholics who want to*

---

[1] Hugh Stott Taylot in *Born Catholics*. Assembled by F. J. Sheed (New York: Sheed & Ward, 1954), pp. 156–57. This is a collection of essays by nineteen distinguished men and women who were "born Catholics" writing (in Mr. Sheed's phrase) about "what their experience of living in the Church has been."

teach in secular colleges and universities. Unless more of the best endowed (with brains and character, not money) young Catholics are encouraged to prepare for and to seek positions in secular education, we will necessarily "abandon the secular colleges to the secularists." This will include all of the public higher institutions which will train the large majority of the future Catholics who will get any higher education. The opportunities are many and the administrators of a secular institution who will not engage personable, scholarly, competent, well-prepared Catholics are relatively hard to find. Doubtless some of them can be found in certain sections of the country in which there are few Catholics, but they will not be easy to find in public institutions anywhere in which there are many Catholic students or a few competent Catholic teachers.

This is not a question of using mere political pressure simply to put Catholics, any Catholics, in educational positions. However, in a state in which the population is, for instance, one-third or one-half Catholic, it seems quite unlikely that there are well-prepared Catholic teachers who would like to teach in the public institutions and who are denied an opportunity. In the past that was quite a regular thing, and in the early years of our public school system this attitude was common not only toward Catholics, but also toward Jews, Unitarians, agnostics, and atheists. Trinitarian Protestantism was essentially the "established religion" of our public school system.[2] Of late years, however, there has apparently been quite a change; in most of the states in which there is a fair proportion of Catholics, the opportunities for Catholics to enter public education are just as good as the opportunities for anyone else.

Those who know the situation best believe that having a fair proportion of such Catholics on the faculties of secular institutions would do more to improve the conditions under which Catholic students live and work, and do more for the standing of the whole Catholic population in a democracy such as ours, than any other one thing that can be done. The difficulty is that there are not enough Catholics who are well prepared for such appointments and who would like to be appointed.

The question may well be asked: How can this situation be changed? It seems clear that if American Catholics are properly to serve the future Catholics of America, and the future of America itself, they must give considerable thought to the problem of promoting, in every legitimate way, the sound, effective preparation of personable, competent, scholarly young Catholics who will seek to enter the faculties of secular institutions; and the thought must be followed by action —encouragement, advice, instruction, perhaps money.

[2] Beale, *op. cit.*, chap. IV.

Dean Taylor, after mentioning the fact that the secular college is "no milieu for the lukewarm Catholic," wrote: "It is almost superfluous to dwell on the opportunities available to the Catholic faculty member of the secular college. . . . Scholarly achievement and professional standing are the necessary prerequisites."[3] He concludes this article (p. 35) with "a plea for the larger intrusion of the Catholic, deliberately, into the secular college and university. That is where the firing line lies. . . . To the extent that you [Catholics] withdraw from the task, to that extent do you abandon the secular institutions to the secularist and to the pagan; to that extent do *you,* not the secularists, increase the secularist climate."

Father John Courtney Murray of Woodstock College considers it "indisputable that the Catholic college and university today ought to be the point of departure for a missionary effort out into the thickening secularist intellectual and spiritual milieu. Their function in the Church . . . [is] completed by discharge of a function in the world and in regard of those who stand without. . . . The crucial institution in the case is the university graduate school."[4] Further on (p. 42) Father Murray says: ". . . there are probably no more

[3] "Catholic Scholars in Secular Universities," *Thought* (New York), March, 1949, p. 32.
[4] "Reversing the Secular Trend," *Thought* (New York), March, 1949, pp. 40–41.

than half a dozen centers of learning in the United States that are essentially determinant of the whole intellectual drift. Here would be the field for which 'missionaries' would be trained. The term is doubtless bad, as suggesting 'evangelization' in some narrow sense. I am thinking of 'presence' in these centers in the only title which admits to presence—ability, learning, scholarly achievement."

However, it would be difficult to overemphasize that the worst possible drawback for the Catholic student, and for Catholics in general, is to have incompetent Catholics in the faculty of secular colleges and universities. There is probably no other single influence more potent in spreading suspicion and distrust of Catholics in education or of Catholic influence on the public life of America. One such teacher can probably cancel the good effect of half a dozen superlative teachers. We should do everything possible to discourage and to eliminate incompetent Catholics in secular education. It seems to me beyond question that anti-Catholicism fares very poorly in institutions in which there are quite a few Catholic teachers; also that the expression of antireligious or anti-Catholic sentiments in the classroom are almost unknown where there are some Catholics in the class, and would probably be totally unknown if the Catholics in the class were properly prepared in information and initiative to rise before the class and ask the teacher for the evidence on which he based an anti-Catholic or antireligious remark. This is a very effective way to stop that sort of thing easily and quickly and would have no unfortunate results for the student in most secular institutions in America.

Of course, the well-informed and competent student will not be disturbed by, or construe as anti-Catholic, every remark that is uncomplimentary to a Catholic person or group; nor will he challenge a properly expressed and legitimate difference of opinion on a controversial topic. The statements that should be openly and frankly challenged are the sort of ignorant or malicious misrepresentations that are now profitably being published by a small group, such as those already mentioned.

Probably the most illuminating document published in recent years concerning Catholics on university faculties with special reference to Catholics on the faculties of secular universities is Chapter II of Father John A. O'Brien's *Catholics and Scholarship*.[5] This volume is a collection of essays written by a number of distinguished Catholics, both priests and laymen. In spite of the fact that it is now seventeen years old, it has no successor, either as a revised edition or a rival volume, and should be read by everyone interested in

[5] (Huntington, Ind., Our Sunday Visitor, 1939).

Catholic education. In Father O'Brien's opinion, "It is scarcely too much to say that the great state and secular universities are the real battlegrounds on which the fate of institutions and the battles of conflicting theories of belief and philosophies of life are fought out."

Father O'Brien quotes two tables from a census.[6]

Without quoting the tables in full, it is sufficient to note that in twenty-eight state universities and colleges covered by this census, the numbers on the faculty from various religious groups were:

State colleges and universities		*State normal schools*
Methodist Episcopal	1152	582
Presbyterian	1098	415
Episcopal	571	128
Baptist	548	257
Congregational	378	140
Catholic	176	70
Jewish	34	8

Thus, the Catholics, the largest religious group in America, had the *smallest* proportion of members on the faculties of state universities and normal schools.

Father O'Brien spent nearly twenty-five years at the university of Illinois as Director of the Newman Club Foundation. He gives a specific statement with regard to the Catholic on the faculty of that great university in a state in which there was a Catholic population of

[6] O. D. Foster, *Religious Census of State Universities, Colleges and Normal Schools in the United States* (Chicago: Council of Church Boards of Education), IV, 9, June, 1921, p. 3.

more than two million at that time, about one fifth of the population of the state. And he testified that the University of Illinois had been presided over by men who were fair and friendly to Catholics. Out of a faculty of 1,101 there were 34 Catholics. "Instead of one out of five, it was one out of 32." Among the full professors of the University there were two Catholics out of 207. "This means that in a state with a Catholic population of more than 2,000,000, Catholics were practically inarticulate on the faculty of the State University to which we contribute in taxes probably more than $1,000,000 a year." Father O'Brien was of the opinion that a similar situation obtained in virtually every state in the union. "Conferences with chaplains at other universities over a long period of years have left no room for doubt that substantially the same situation prevails at other state universities throughout the country." This situation has improved, but there is not yet anything like proper "proportional representation" of Catholics among the various religious groups in the population of the United States.

Not only were there few Catholics found in the faculties of public higher institutions, but the boards which control them were similarly constituted. Father O'Brien reports that at Illinois, "the Board consists of nine members chosen at a general election by the voters of the State, with the Governor and Superintendent of

Public Instruction as *ex officio* members. . . . The University has been in existence about seventy-five years and hundreds of trustees have served during that period. Now the amazing and incredible fact is that during all those years there had never been a single Catholic on the Board of Trustees down to 1935. This excepts the case of one Catholic governor of the state who was merely an *ex officio* member." His conclusion is: "We seem to have a rare genius for aloofness from the public tax-supported institutions which are largely directing scholarly thought in America. What is the result of this policy of isolation and aloofness? It has cost us dearly in prestige, in influence upon scholarship, and in public opinion."

Father O'Brien speaks of "the true weakness of Catholics in the United States" as follows: "Among those who are creating public consciousness in contemporary America, for better or for worse, singularly few stand inside the pale of the Church." Here it may be well to call attention to the message of His Holiness, Pope Pius XII, to the World Congress of Pax Romana at Amsterdam, Holland, in 1950, in which he urged the Catholics, scholars, and intellectuals of the world to affect the thought of those around them on the contemporary problems of their society. Father O'Brien is doubtless correct in saying that if the Catholics of America wish ever to exert their proportional influence on the public consciousness of America they should start by making every legitimate effort to increase the number of scholarly and competent Catholics on the faculties of secular institutions of higher education in our country.

I believe there is nothing which the Catholics of America could do more effectively to improve the public standing of Catholics among our citizenship (and to make more difficult the appeal of such writers as Mr. Blanshard and Professor Nichols and their followers) than to promote this increase. Further, it seems plain to those who know the situation that, next to the activity of the Catholic student chaplains, having a proper proportion of competent Catholic teachers in various departments would contribute more in various ways toward preserving the faith of the Catholic students in these institutions than anything else that could be done for them.

The situation has been much improved in recent decades. A Catholic scientist of long experience on the faculty of a public university in a section of the South in which there are relatively few Catholics reported that when he was appointed to the university many years ago he was the first Catholic on the faculty. And only once in the over forty years that he was on this faculty was the subject of his religion ever mentioned. That occurred when this professor's activity attracted some attention and an anti-Catholic agitator said: "It will not be long before the Pope takes over the university." Following this outburst the president of the institution asked him, in a joking manner, "When is the Pope coming over to take my job?"

In the early days of his professorship there was one small mission church in the community and about one hundred Catholics, with three or four Catholic students in the university. Today the community has a church, an elementary school, a convent, a hospital, and a Newman Club student center at the university. There are two resident priests, one in charge of the student center. Sisters are conducting a school in the hospital. There are daily Masses and three Masses on Sunday, each one filling the church. And about three hundred Catholic students attend the university. Interestingly enough, this number is reported to be only about 5 per cent of the student body, but only two denominations outrank the Catholics in percentage of students—the Baptist, with over 40 per cent, and the Methodist, with about 35 per cent. There are now twelve Catholic members of the university faculty.

There is some anti-Catholicism on the faculty according to this professor's report, but largely in the departments of history and philosophy. Like most other similarly experienced Catholics he sees no reason to fear sending a Catholic boy or girl to this university *provided the student comes adequately prepared.*

The opinion is widespread that a great many Catholic students enter secular higher education very badly prepared, not because it is difficult to prepare them, but because very little attention has been given to providing the preparation.

A Catholic professor in another university writes that an important factor which "accounts for much of the prejudices and ignorances on the other side" is "the scarcity of Catholic lay scholars and the provincial narrowness of the relatively few who are available." Naturally he would like to see "a greater number of competent Catholic scholars in secular education. . . . More often than not, the informed Catholic scholar is the best hope and the sole anchor which both Catholic and non-Catholic students find in their hunger for spiritual values in an otherwise almost completely secularized and pagan environment."

A Catholic professor in one of the great secular universities of the country, who was entirely educated in Catholic schools and colleges and who had taught in them for a number of years before going into secular higher education, believes that if the position of Catholics in education and "the whole intellectual field in this country is to improve, something [has to be done that is] positive, crusading, optimistic, rather than afraid, taking shelter, trying to avoid contamination. . . . Facing the secular world of thought may be a tough experience for the Catholic (especially, perhaps, if he has been largely educated inside the Catholic walls) and yet again the danger, the fears, the misgivings, the oppressive atmosphere may be less if more Catholics . . . keep saying that the issue has to be met and can be met." He supports the practically unanimous belief of Catholics in secular education that there is not "much bigotry or anti-Catholic feeling," but rather the danger is "the neutral, historical, anthropological, scientific and merely descriptive attitude toward religion and morals which largely prevails in our world-tempered universities." But he continues: "I can't help thinking all the time how much Catholics *need* the outside world and to come to some kind of terms with it. . . . I am glad to see young priests come here to study, because I think they are going back to improve things in the Catholic colleges." He reports an impression of which I have had confirming experiences a number of times, that the personal and professional handicaps of the Catholic teacher are largely nonexistent. "For the moment he has some advantages. Large secular universities frequently [want] qualified Catholics, and not so many Catholics yet are professionally qualified."

I have known in my professional life department heads, deans, and presidents in secular colleges and universities who desired to add competent Catholics to their faculties. I have never known of a well-prepared Catholic teacher who wanted to go into secular education who failed to find a satisfactory opportunity. I have known of one or two quite incompetent Catholics in secular education who failed to get the promotions or advances in salary which they desired, and one or two who were dropped for incompetence and who protested loudly against the "anti-Catholicism" or the "pro-Communism" of which they were the victims. I knew one who was dropped by a Catholic department chairman, serving under a Catholic president, who immediately did everything possible to stir up quite a bit of wondering about how such a "devout Catholic" could be so mistreated by Catholics in public education.

In speaking of the Catholics on the faculties of secular universities, one of the most eminent members of this group writes: "The important thing is that they should be not only competent, but well trained in the field in which they offer themselves and ready to grow and able to wear their difference with ease." Such a person "learns to respect differences; I think he is impressed by the good will of so many people. Conversely, his friends come to think of the Catholic faith as something held by people whom they know and like and who share so many of their common interests."

A Catholic scientist, who spent seven years as an

undergraduate and graduate student in secular institutions and who has had thirty-one years as a teacher in public colleges, writes: "Handicaps for either study or work in secular colleges are slight for any Catholic who is well enough informed to be safely allowed to go 'out into the world,' and who can live harmoniously with fellow men." The chief source of danger, he believes, are the "so-called broad-minded instructors" in some departments "who in many cases are not at heart anti-Catholic, but have acquired notions, not knowledge, that sum up to a complete misunderstanding in regard to Catholicism and Catholics." He blames the small number of Catholic scholars in secular education to the "miserably few Catholic students who are disposed, or can be induced, to pursue graduate studies, a requisite for successful teaching in these colleges. . . . Perhaps it may be necessary to promote this idea in Catholic colleges as well as in secular colleges if any impressive progress is to be made. Certainly Catholic scholars in both are in a position to exert the most potent influence in this direction on young Catholic students under their care."

Another Catholic scientist, educated exclusively in public institutions, who has taught thirty-four years in public education in six different states and who has been a visiting instructor in three Catholic colleges and six non-Catholic private and public colleges and universities, writes that he has "encountered nothing unusual in the way of treatment due to my religion." He feels "very strongly that Catholics should take their share of the task of public education. But I feel equally strongly that public school teaching is no occupation for indifferent Catholics, or indeed, for that matter, for any indifferent Christian. . . . A lukewarm Catholic is a double liability in public education—first, to his faith, and second, to our way of life."

Of course, all incompetent teachers should be eliminated as rapidly as possible from any type of educational institution. But incompetence is a relative term and people differ as to what kinds of incompetence should be operative in bringing about a separation of the teacher from his job. Doubtless, basically there should be in every institution appropriate machinery for carefully examining each new teacher while he is still on a temporary appointment—that is, before he has the security of tenure in the institution. A careful decision should be made by the proper authorities, preferably a committee, as to whether the teacher is satisfactory *for that institution*. During any temporary or probationary appointment a teacher is quite literally only a potential applicant for reappointment and failure to reappoint him is simply a failure to give him a job for which he is an applicant and should not be treated as a *dismissal*.

In these days of the tremendous shortage of teachers in all kinds of schools, there are probably going to be more and somewhat incompetent teachers hired and retained than would be the situation if an ample supply of good teachers were available. However, we are not concerned in this particular book with discussing the general problem of selecting or retaining teachers. I simply want to emphasize the fact that there is probably no one item in this whole situation which can do more damage to Catholics in education or to American Catholics in general than the appointment or retention of incompetent, uncouth, unsatisfactory (to their colleagues, the administration, or the students) Catholic classroom teachers.

A few years ago a group of six educators had the responsibility of making a nomination for a very important educational post. Two of the six were Catholics. There were a great many names submitted to this committee and at the first meeting of the committee it was noticed that many Catholics were recommended. As the first Catholic name appeared for consideration, someone, not one of the Catholic members (without the slightest indication of any prejudice for or against the person named), mentioned the fact that this man was a well-known Catholic. Immediately the two Catholic members of the committee took the position, explicitly and emphatically, that they would agree to no

Catholic nomination for this position unless it was recognized by the committee that such a person was an outstanding educator, eminently qualified for the position in the opinion of the whole group, and that no one was going to get the position, or gain the slightest advantage toward getting it, from the fact that he was a Catholic. It seems to me that this is the only sound position which Catholics in education can take, or which Catholics working to place Catholics in education can take. Poorly prepared Catholics, or Catholics with poor personal qualifications, do succeed in getting into positions in education as well as similar people of other religious beliefs or of none; and they should be treated exactly the same way regardless of the quality of their religious devotion.

There are some, and I have known a few, in the institutions in which I have taught, who blame their Catholicism for anything which happens to them which they dislike, and this attitude is not confined to Catholics. An amusing situation once arose in an institution in which I was at work when, in the course of my responsibility, I took action against a Catholic colleague who was thoroughly displeased by my attitude. At precisely the same time, a distinguished Jewish colleague of mine denied a certain teaching assignment much desired by a young Jewish teacher. Then the institution was treated to the experience, coincidentally, of O'Neill being accused of anti-Catholicism and his Jewish colleague of anti-Semitism by two disappointed teachers who were judged professionally unsatisfactory by the two members of the faculty who had the primary responsibility for maintaining professional standards in their areas.

Such a situation is most unfortunate for the disgruntled Catholic who creates it, and for all Catholics in secular education. It doubtless also works to the disadvantage of Catholics in various other situations throughout the country.

5

Secular Education and Catholic Scholarship

Since the increase in the number of well-prepared Catholics on the faculties of the secular colleges and universities attended by large numbers of Catholic students (notably the public institutions) is widely recognized as a matter of great importance, and since this change is largely dependent on the increased production of excellent Catholic scholars who are fully prepared to take important posts in secular institutions, it seems pertinent in this book to discuss briefly the problem of American Catholic scholarship.

Comments of various kinds concerning the lack of distinguished Catholic scholars in proportion to the Catholic population of the country have been too common in the last few decades to allow of any doubt as to their truth. Sometimes these comments are phrased as attacks against the Catholic Church, viz., that the

Catholic Church is opposed to sound scholarship or that the doctrines of the Church are not consonant with scientific investigation. This charge, of course, when honestly made, is based on simple ignorance of the history of the Catholic Church through the centuries. Such ignorance must be due in many instances to culpable avoidance of information. The more impressive statements concerning the relative or proportional lack of distinction of Catholic scholarship are to be found in considerable profusion in the writings of distinguished Catholics, lay and clerical, in Catholic publications of various sorts. Many of these comments come directly from eminent members of the faculties of Catholic colleges and universities; they are not in any way criticisms of Catholic *doctrine*.

As Father John A. O'Brien of Notre Dame University, one of the noted critics of the record of achievement of American Catholics in the field of scholarship, has written: "The Church is not the issue. She has been the mother of learning, art, and culture throughout the centuries." [1]

The opinion of the relative lack of distinguished Catholic scholarship in America is so widespread and often so carefully documented in Catholic publications that it seems inadvisable to take up space simply to prove the prevalence of the opinion. However, some

[1] *Op. cit.*, p. 62.

exposition of the nature and extent of this weakness, the principal causes and possible cures, seem thoroughly desirable and potentially helpful to the Church, to all American Catholics, and to American society in general.

While admittedly the situation has changed somewhat in the last twenty years, the statement, in 1935, of Father X. LeBuffe, S.J., then editor of *Thought,* is still held by many to be sound and relevant. He laid the "characteristic disinterestedness of Catholics in science squarely to the lack of scholarly outlook on the part of the clergy. Most priests do not realize that 'priestly work' is not necessarily parochial. The Church has need for scholars in every field. Some of them must be men who are free from parochial responsibilities and activities. The common attitude on the part of the vast majority of American clergy is to penalize priests who do not follow the usual routine of parish work. This is equally true in religious communities. Teaching is thought so much of that additional classes are easily found for every member of the institutional staff. Men and women who have ability and liking for research are sidetracked into executive or even parochial positions. The obstacles to developing a research program in our schools are two: One is a psychological attitude towards anything that does not come under the heading of what is now understood as 'priestly work'; and the other is the terrific barrier of indifference on the part of superiors." [2]

Teachers of wide experience in public colleges and universities will doubtless agree that Catholic institutions are not the only ones that schedule teaching loads for most faculty members that make much sound research and scholarly publishing nearly impossible.

Two very obvious partial explanations of this lack are, first, the comparative absence of money and leisure among the vast majority of the Catholic population, this vast majority being quite clearly descendants of relatively recent immigrants, most of whom did not, of course, come to America with vast stores of wealth; and, the second, the very large proportion of the Catholic young men who are best equipped by nature to be distinguished scholars, who instead of devoting their lives to scholarship enter the Church as priests and after ordination are busy throughout most of their lives in the various parishes of the country attending to the needs of tremendous congregations. Or else they become teachers in understaffed schools and colleges and then go through many, many years of what has been referred to as "the drudgery of unrelieved years of pedagogy."

[2] Quoted by Father John S. O'Brien, *op. cit.*, p. 14 from *The Tabloid Scientist* (New York: Fordham University, Catholic Round Table of Science), February 1, 1935.

It is, of course, possible to use the phrase "Catholic scholar" to mean at least two different types of scholar. First, it means a scholar (in any field, working in any institution or in none) who is a Catholic. This, I believe, is the most common use of the phrase "Catholic scholar" in this country, especially when it is used by a secular writer or a secular publication of any kind, and frequently by Catholics working in secular institutions of higher education. It is the meaning of the phrase "Catholic scholar" used in this book. Here, a "Catholic scholar" simply means a scholar who is a Catholic, as one might speak of a Catholic doctor, a Catholic lawyer, or a Catholic athlete.

The second legitimate—though, I believe, much less common—use of the term means a scholar who is not only a Catholic, but who is writing on a strictly Catholic subject with apparently the assumption that such a person is well-trained in Catholic institutions, and in Catholic doctrine, theological and philosophical.

I am of the opinion that as of today Catholic scholarship, in the meaning of either definition, does not have the reputation which it deserves.

Most of the Catholic scholars are doubtless to be found in the faculties of Catholic colleges and universities. While I have never been a member of the faculty in any Catholic institution, I have had close contact with the work of doctoral candidates in the universities of Wisconsin and Michigan, and Northwestern University, and am familiar with doctor's theses from other secular institutions. I have never had close contact with the work of graduate students in Catholic universities, but I am quite familiar with Ph.D. theses from some of the Catholic universities, and a number of them are the equal of any, and superior to many, of the Ph.D. theses I have known from secular universities.

In my opinion, the lack of scholarly recognition is largely due to a situation which was deplored by Father P. H. Yancey, S.J., of Springhill College, at a meeting of the Catholic Round Table of Science on December 27, 1934.[3] The remedy emphasized by Father Yancey was "closer affiliation with local research groups, state academies of science and other organizations of scientists." Catholic scholarship would have a much better reputation than it has today if the scholarly work of the faculties of the Catholic colleges and universities were to appear more frequently side by side with the output of the faculties of non-Catholic institutions at the meetings of learned societies and in learned journals. Dean Taylor of Princeton remarks along the same line: "The necessity to prove oneself extends beyond the campus to the professional and learned societies, the professional and scholarly publi-

[3] *Ibid.*

cations. Here, especially must we be on guard against segregation." [4]

In other words, great advantage would accrue to the reputation of Catholic institutions, Catholic scholars, and to the Catholic Church in America if the scholars in Catholic institutions of higher education would mingle much more freely with the regular professional groups to which they belong by the nature of their professional interest—the groups that have no religious qualifications, that are interested only in the scholarly work of their members.

The comparative aloofness from the larger learned societies of the United States on the part of faculty members of Catholic institutions has a number of unfortunate effects. It not only plays its part in depriving the current Catholic scholars of the reputation as scholars to which they are properly entitled, but it operates doubtless to keep down the number of distinguished scholars of the future. While definite proof is not available, it seems reasonable to suppose that the fact that only a relatively small number of American Catholics have achieved distinction as scholars must have a depressing effect on Catholic students who might otherwise plan a career leading to scholarly distinction.

Probably the most complete and up-to-date discus-

[4] *Thought,* March 1949, p. 33.

sion of American Catholic scholarship is *The American Catholic and the Intellectual Life* by the Reverend John Tracy Ellis. In this article Father Ellis discusses the principal causes that have "produced in American Catholics generally, as well as in the intellectuals, a pervading spirit of separatism from their fellow citizens of other religious faiths. They have suffered from the timidity that characterizes minority groups, from the effects of a ghetto mentality they have themselves fostered, and, too, from a sense of inferiority induced by their consciousness of the inadequacy of Catholic scholarship. . . . The chief blame, I firmly believe, lies with Catholics themselves . . . in their failure to have measured up to the responsibilities of the incomparable tradition of Catholic learning of which they are the direct heirs." [5]

The unfortunate attitude in America toward the intellectual life is not to be found only among Catholics. Father Ellis lists a number of learned commentators, both Catholic and non-Catholic, who have written on the American attitude toward intellectuals. He writes that "their analysis reveals a universal agreement that the situation of the intellectual in the United

[5] *Thought* (New York), XXX, 118, Autumn, 1955. The author is Professor of Church History at the Catholic University of America. The substance of this article was read as a paper at the meeting of the Catholic Commission on Intellectual and Cultural Affairs, at Maryville College, St. Louis, Missouri, May 14, 1955. Quoted with permission.

States has been, and is at the present time, deplorable." He quotes Henry Steele Commager that the American intellectuals "have failed to enlist the great mass of their countrymen in the common cultural and intellectual enterprise necessary for the Republic's progress and security." After quoting de Tocqueville (1825) and Brownson (1853) on the then prevalent lack of enthusiasm for intellectual achievement in America, Father Ellis observes: "Nor have matters greatly improved since the time of de Tocqueville and Brownson, for it has been our own generation that has given birth to the terms 'brain trusters' and 'eggheads' to designate the popular concept of professors who have descended from Mount Olympus to engage actively in the realm of public affairs. In this respect, I regret to say, I can see no appreciable difference between the attitudes assumed by American Catholics and those commonly held among their fellow countrymen of other religious faiths. . . . In that—as in so many other ways—the Catholics are, and have been, thoroughly American, and they have shown no more marked disposition to foster scholarship and to honor intellectual achievement than have any other group."

However, this general situation in our country does not excuse the low state of Catholic scholarship. In spite of the fact that American Catholic intellectuals, as Father Ellis observes, "are in possession of the oldest, wisest, and most sublime tradition of learning that the world has ever known," he reports various studies which have shown that "in no single phase of national life have Catholics made the contribution to leadership which might be expected of them, but if there be any exception to this general statement, it most certainly lies in the field of business." This general failure is the result of a variety of contributing factors, which help to explain, but which taken together do not excuse the Catholic record. Father Ellis mentions among the contributing factors the following:

(1) The "deep anti-Catholic prejudice by the original English settlers in the early seventeenth century" that is referred to by Ray and Myers.[6] He quotes Professor Arthur M. Schlesinger, Sr., of Harvard, "one of the outstanding authorities in American social history," as saying to him: "I regard the bias against your Church as the most persistent prejudice in the history of the American people." Father Ellis continues: "Any notion that this sentiment was only a part of our past has been thoroughly dispelled by the substantial support afforded to groups like 'Protestants and Other Americans United for the Separation of Church and State' since World War II." While this prejudice was

---

[6] Sister Mary Augustina Ray, *American Opinion of Catholicism in the Eighteenth Century* (New York: Columbia University Press, 1936); Gustavus Myers, *History of Bigotry in the United States* (New York: Random House, 1943).

widespread and vigorous until well along in the nineteenth century, it had been dying out from shortly after the Civil War until Protestants and Other Americans United for the Separation of Church and State began to organize, preserve, and distribute misinformation and misrepresentation about the Constitution of the United States, the Catholic Church, and the beliefs, practices, and hopes of American Catholics. The nature and longevity of anti-Catholic bias in America has been reported by numerous non-Catholic scholars of distinction in American social history, particularly Billington, Beale, and Curti.[7] Dr. Billington, in the Foreword to his *The Protestant Crusade,*[8] pays a fine tribute to Professor Schlesinger, under whom he began his graduate study of American nativism, which later resulted in his Ph.D thesis on this subject, and in his book just mentioned.

(2) The large proportion of relatively recent immigrant ancestry of most American Catholics in the last century meant the absence of the generations needed for the accumulation of traditions of culture, plus the possession of wealth and leisure—essentials for the most notable achievements in the field of scholarship. From about 1820 to 1920 "the Church was faced with the staggering task of absorbing an estimated 9,317,000

[7] See footnote 9, chap. III.
[8] *Op. cit.*

immigrants of its Faith. We do not need to be told what the immigrant status implied by way of poverty, hardship, yes, and even illiteracy. Most of us learned it from tales told by our grandparents within the intimacy of the family circle." [9]

(3) The failure to start children in "the habit of reading" in the home is a potent cause of the failure of Catholics, as well as other Americans generally, to achieve greater distinction in the intellectual life. There is considerable evidence available to show in books and articles on education, and in almost universal comment on the effect of television on school children, to indicate that now and in the immediate future the problem of starting the reading habit in childhood must be largely the responsibility of parents in their direction of child activities out of school.

However, Father Ellis finds a partial exception to this general situation. He remarks that Catholics have distinguished themselves "in the native penchant for making money," and cites a number of published studies and the activity of the students in his seminar, as

[9] One of my grandmothers could not read or write because in her childhood and youth in Ireland the English law made it a criminal offense to teach a Catholic child to read and there were not always enough "hedge masters" to serve all parts of the country. They and their "hedge school" had to operate in secret and were suppressed wherever they could be discovered. The hedge masters were usually priests and laymen who had succeeded in getting abroad to study (J. M. O'Neill). See Donald Attwater, *The Catholic Dictionary* (New York: Macmillan, 1943), p. 238; and Robert I. Gannon, S.J., "The Hedge Master," *After Black Coffee* (New York: McMullen, 1947), pp. 85–91.

indicating that, "relatively speaking, Catholic business leadership on a national scale [in the 1940's] ran ahead of leadership in national politics, and this made the showing by Catholics who had attained national recognition through productive scholarship seem insignificant by comparison."

In connection with these remarks Father Ellis has a footnote (Number 24, p. 364) which says in part: "It was found, for example, that there were 171 Catholic businessmen in positions of the first rank . . . for the years investigated; whereas in the entire history of the country there have been only five Catholic members of the Supreme Court, and fourteen members of the Presidents' cabinets out of a total of 301 men since 1789, and ten of these were appointed since 1933."

Of course, Father Ellis is not taking the position that the small number of Catholics on the Court and in the Cabinets is a result of the general failure to win distinction in "scholarship." Such distinction is obviously not one of the requirements for such Presidential appointments (though it would not be a bar). I suppose that no one who is well acquainted with the social history of the United States and with the characteristic features of our current pluralistic society could seriously and honestly contend that the Presidents would at any time have had any difficulty in finding the required number of Catholic businessmen and lawyers who were at least as well qualified as the non-Catholic businessmen and lawyers who were almost invariably chosen. But only five Presidents out of thirty-three have ever appointed a Catholic to the Supreme Court. A sixth, Taft, promoted one to chief justiceship. However, the explanation of the paucity of Catholics in Cabinet and Supreme Court is beyond the purview of this book.

(4) The pressure of administrative work, parish duties and classroom teaching leaves little time for the concerns of scholarship. In regard to "the role played by the clerical leaders of the American Church [the bishops and the heads of the various religious orders]," Father Ellis reminds us that "the vast majority of them have been men of their own generation, reflecting . . . the predominant attitudes and prevailing tendencies of their time." They are, and have to be, competent administrators; whether they are productive scholars must be a secondary consideration. However, Father Ellis joins many other commentators in regretting that "the pressing tasks of administration leave so little time and leisure to these spiritual superiors for a more active participation and effective encouragement to intellectual concerns." There follows an overemphasis on the "professional and vocational aspects of higher education." This obviously leads to the frequently mentioned demands of too much time of priests and sisters *who*

are potentially distinguished scholars in the burdensome routine of parish duties and teaching. This fits in nicely with Father Ellis' pleasure in reporting: "The percentage of lay teachers at every level of American Catholic education has been steadily increasing of late years, and is especially true of the colleges and universities. For example, in the academic year 1952–1953 laymen composed 73.8 per cent of the entire faculty of the Catholic University of America, and in the same year of 753 members of the teaching staff of Marquette University, 700 were drawn from the laity. . . . Catholic scholarship and learning, generally speaking, would be improved by giving to the laity more of a voice in shaping the educational policy and in the active administration of the Catholic colleges and universities of the United States."

(5) An additional reason is that the Catholic universities have been trying to compete with the secular universities in expanding curricula to cover various vocational and professional subjects, and neglecting too much of the great Catholic tradition in education, illustrated by the fact that the revival in scholastic philosophy "found its most enthusiastic and hard-working friends on the campuses of the University of Chicago, the University of Virginia, Princeton University, and St. John's College, Annapolis."

(6) Father Ellis deplores "as a major defect in Cath-

olic higher education . . . the numerous and compet-
ing graduate schools, none of which is adequately
endowed, and few of which have the trained personnel,
the equipment in libraries and laboratories, and the
professional wage scales to warrant their undertakings.
The result is a perpetuation of mediocrity and the
draining away from each other of the strength that is
necessary if really superior achievements are to be
attained." He endorses "planning for Catholic higher
education on a national scale" to include not only the
universities but also the more than two hundred Catholic colleges. He fears financial bankruptcy for these
institutions, but thinks that nothing else will end the
"senseless duplication of effort and the wasteful prolif-
eration" now observable in Catholic higher education.

Anyone interested in a fundamental understanding
of the present status of Catholic scholarship in America
should read this whole article of thirty-eight large
pages. It is the best and most complete discussion on
the subject that has appeared since Father John A.
O'Brien's little book was published in 1939.[10] Like that
book this article strengthens the argument that Catholic scholarship and Catholic contribution to the intellectual life of America would be improved by more
contact between Catholic and non-Catholic scholars,
and especially by more Catholic scholars of unques-

[10] *Op. cit.*

tioned competence in the faculties of secular universities.

Most Catholics who have had many years of experience in secular institutions of higher education seem to believe that increasing the number of Catholic teachers on the faculties of secular institutions would be beneficial in various ways, not only to American Catholics, but to American society as a whole.

In recent months I have had communications, oral or written, from a large number of Catholic teachers in secular colleges and universities. They are unanimous in the opinion that the explanation of the few Catholics to be found in these positions in comparison with the number of Catholics in the total population is not anti-Catholicism on the part of those who select and appoint members of secular faculties; in fact, it seems apparent that they have never known of an instance of that sort in secular higher education in this country.

Doubtless years ago there were such instances. However, I believe it would be difficult to find any of them in recent decades. What, then, is the explanation? The explanation given by most of them is the scarcity of really qualified Catholics who are interested in such positions. There is considerable opinion that many of the presidents and deans, and other administrative officers of secular colleges and universities would be glad to have a larger number of Catholics in their institutions, many of which have tremendous numbers of Catholic students. A thoroughly sound estimate, which is all we can have since, apparently, the actual statistics have never been gathered, is that in some colleges and universities it would be quite normal to find roughly one fourth of the students Catholics and about one twentieth of the faculty. This is partly because the Catholics do not apply; the administrators do not know about Catholic candidates.

One man, in further explanation, said that, if a graduate of a Catholic college applies, the administrator in the secular institution, in looking over the applicant's recommendations from his teachers in the Catholic institutions, is reading recommendations written by men whom he does not know. He has never met them in learned societies, he has never read their articles in the journals in which he has read the articles of other men in their fields, and he simply has no basis for knowing the weight to be attached to the recommendations of these professors. This cannot be assigned to prejudice. I think anyone who has had the responsibility of going over the recommendations of scores of candidates for positions in secular institutions, as I had for many decades, will admit that the most effective recommendation comes from a person whom one knows well and knows to be a frank, conscientious, and competent judge of young teachers; in other words, the administrator knows when he sees the signature that he can be guided by the statements in the recommendation. In that case, almost any administrator will follow that recommendation and disregard those from men about whom he knows nothing.

And the best answer to this situation seems to be for Catholic teachers, administrators, and scholars (not mutually exclusive terms) to mingle more freely with non-Catholics in their respective fields, and further there should be a great deal more encouragement of some of the brightest of the Catholic youth to enter secular graduate schools as the best approach to appointment to a secular faculty.

If a Catholic graduate of a Catholic college should become interested in teaching in secular higher education, he would presumably be well enough grounded in Catholic doctrine and history so as not to be disturbed by the fellow students and teachers whom he will meet in secular institutions, and he and his advisers should consider the advantages of a secular university noted for its strength in the particular field in which the student wishes to work, and go to the secular university for his graduate studies and his doctor's degree.

The need for more Catholics with good reputations as scholars on secular faculties, especially in institutions with thousands of Catholic students, is universally recognized by Catholics who have been close to this situation. However, I have no evidence that the specific remedy recommended as advisable in many cases above (that graduates of Catholic colleges go to secular graduate schools) is so widely endorsed. I do know that it is recommended (not for all, of course, but for some of the best) by a number of sincere and devoted Catholics, some of whom have been both students and teachers in Catholic higher education.

From such a position the young Ph.D. could step relatively easily into a beginning position in some secular institution—where he is very badly needed in the opinion of practically every experienced commentator on this situation.

Father John A. O'Brien, in the book above mentioned, Chapter III, comments briefly on a number of publications which will substantiate much of what is said above concerning Catholic scholarship.[11]

[11] Anyone who would like to read some of the earlier writing on this subject should see at least the following books: George N. Shuster, "Have We Any Scholars?" *America* (New York), August 15, 1925; also by the same author, *The Catholic Spirit in America* (New York: Dial Press, 1927); K. F. Herzfeld, of the Catholic University of America, "Scientific Research and Religion," *Commonweal* (New York), March 20, 1929. When he wrote this article, Dr. Herzfeld was a member of the faculty of Johns Hopkins University. See also Richard Muttkowski, "What Is Research?" *America* (New York), June 29, 1929; Father John Tracy Ellis, "Catholic Scholarship," *Thought* (New York), Autumn, 1955. An editorial comment in the *Monitor* (San Francisco) May 26, 1928, concerns the lack of Catholic laymen who would be fitted to teach many subjects in the great secular universities.

It seems true that a large proportion of the Catholics of the country who are well qualified to take professorships in secular institutions are Catholic priests. Also many lay scholars teach in Catholic colleges and universities. The opinion is sometimes expressed that that is where they should be—that the place for a Catholic scholar is in a Catholic institution. As is already clear to anyone who has read this far in this book, I dissent, and most of the Catholics who have been at work in the secular institutions of the country agree in that dissent.

Of course Catholic scholars should be at work also in Catholic universities, but those of us who know well the situation in secular institutions believe almost without exception that there is a great need for Catholics on the faculties of secular institutions, where will be found the majority of the Catholics who are going to be the college-educated Catholics of the future.

There have been some illuminating instances in which secular institutions have tried to get Catholic scholars to take distinguished positions and have failed to attract them because, for some reason not disclosed, the Catholics preferred to stay in Catholic institutions. In one instance, with the details of which I was quite familiar, a number of years ago the chairman of a philosophy department (incidentally, the son of a Lutheran minister) and the president of a college (a

Unitarian) went deliberately about the business of bringing into the faculty and the Department of Philosophy a thoroughly trained, competent Catholic to teach scholastic philosophy. They naturally thought such teachers could be found among the graduates of the best Catholic graduate schools and asked some of them for suggestions, which they received. After careful investigation they made offers to a number of highly trained Catholic laymen. A few declined. Why some of them declined the offer, I do not know. I am confident that it was not because they received a higher salary in the Catholic institution. But I do know that one of them declined because at the same time he was considering an offer to go from the great secular university in which he was then teaching to a relatively small, but excellent, Catholic college.

Regardless of the effect which his teaching can have on the students of the small Catholic college in which he is now teaching, I am confident that it was a great loss to the Church and to thousands of students (especially Catholics) in secular education when he declined the offer of the secular institution to accept the offer of a Catholic college. I am not saying that he was *wrong* in his decision because I know nothing about just what motives prompted the decision he made. I am only regretting the loss to a large number of Catholic students and to the interests of the Catholics of

America that this particular young man is not teaching in a great secular institution.

It is sometimes said that a Catholic professor in a secular university has to be very careful of what he says and what he does, that he must "tread softly" and not "inflict his religion on his students." It seems fairly sound doctrine that no teacher should "inflict" his religion on his students or his politics or any of his beliefs or theories. It would be unfortunate if his treatment of even his own subject could be properly character- ized as "inflicting it on his students." But the idea that a Catholic professor in secular education should be more cautious and circumspect than a non-Catholic and tread softly in order that his colleagues and stu- dents will not know that he is an active and conscien- tious Catholic is exactly opposite to the opinion of practically every Catholic professor from whom I have heard in connection with this matter—and that is a large number.

An interesting comment made some twenty years ago, and obviously to be somewhat discounted at the present time, is to be found in O'Brien.[12] There Dr. George N. Kramer, writing under the pen name of Justin E. West, writes: "Pay for services in most of our Catholic institutions of higher learning is notori- ously low . . . too low to enable anyone to engage in

[12] *Op. cit.*, pp. 55, 56.

research," that to become a scholar and produce sound research requires leisure, money, and proper facilities for whatever work the scholar is undertaking, and that is the reason, or a large part of the reason, for the scarcity of Catholic scholars. He continues: "The natural reaction is to reply that if Catholic institutions do not afford the leisure, the facilities, and the means for scholarship, the reasonable thing to do is to affiliate with state or secular institutions that do offer these essentials. Unfortunately that is exactly what our Catholic students are doing. The youth who look to a life of learning and research are entering the halls of secular education and can we blame them? But it may be urged, these students will ultimately become scholars, augmenting the list of representative Catholics, filling the dire need of which Father O'Brien has written. The answer is that they positively will not. They will be secular trained and, while they may profess and continue to practice the Catholic religion, which becomes doubtful, they cannot be called Catholic scholars. They must be products of Catholic institutions, well grounded in Catholic principles and imbued with the spirit as well as the forms of the Catholic philosophy."

I trust that today the author of these lines would not be quite so sure that men trained in secular graduate schools could not be called Catholic scholars. And that it would be doubtful that they would even continue to be Catholics. It seems that the record of many Catholics who are graduates of the secular graduate schools and of the great universities have demonstrated the error which lurks in the above quoted lines. There are many (but not nearly enough) exemplary Catholics teaching in the graduate schools of this country in secular education. It is interesting to note, for instance, that the deans of the graduate schools of both Harvard University and Princeton University are Catholics. And it seems strange, or it would if the statement were made today, that graduates of a Catholic college entering the graduate schools of Princeton and Harvard and many other secular institutions would be endangering their Catholic religion.

I trust that these lines that I have just quoted from Dr. Kramer will be read with the date in mind. Such a remark today, I think, would be a serious reflection upon the Catholic colleges of the country as well as the secular graduate schools. The closing sentences of this article entitled, "Scholars Have Stomachs," seems to be a very appropriate passage to follow with a quotation from Father O'Brien written many years later. The closing of Dr. Kramer's article reads, "We may speak of the inarticulate working classes. There are rising up champions on every hand to defend them, but what about the inarticulate, unorganized, abused, overworked, underpaid, and underprivileged Catholic college professors. There have risen up multitudes to scoff at him, and he is without honor among his own people. That is why, from the standpoint of Catholic scholarship, we are barren unwatered trees."

Father John A. O'Brien, in an article entitled "Developing Catholic Scholars," [13] mentions as important handicaps the heavy teaching load in Catholic institutions, due, of course, to a lack of money, and the frequent "indifference and even latent hostility of superiors" to research and scholarship; due also, doubtless, to lack of sufficient money to hire a large enough staff of teachers to promote both teaching and scholarship.

Also the lack of suitable facilities, laboratory, equipment, and libraries is due almost exclusively to a lack of sufficient funds; and finally, adequate salaries to hire a sufficient number of properly trained lay teachers and scholars.

In fact in this article Father O'Brien's whole explanation of the present relatively small amount of sound scholarship coming from the Catholic educational institutions boils down to a lack of money. However, one item—the absence of intimate participation by the faculty members in Catholic institutions in the work of the various learned societies and of attendance at their meetings as has already been suggested—doubtless explains the absence of the reputation which *pres-*

[13] *America* (New York), June 7, 1947.

ent Catholic scholarship actually produced and the Catholic educational institutions really deserve.

But perhaps what is most interesting in this article is a suggestion of something to be done; if this were really worked out, it would mean either more money or diversion of present money to increase salaries, of the lay staff particularly.

Two paragraphs should be quoted: "*Organization Necessary.* An organization of teachers to secure equal bargaining power through collective action is long overdue. Individuals won't get much by acting alone except perhaps the speedy release, but organized teachers will be able to wring from our school administrators approximations of the three objectives to which all workers are entitled: adequate pay, reasonable security, and satisfactory working conditions. We hope this doesn't sound unduly radical, Utopian, or facetious. We are in deadly earnest. Members of our hierarchy have come out in support of the struggles of the CIO to secure higher wages for automotive workers, have backed the AF of L in its efforts to lift the wages of truck drivers, applauded the endeavors of John L. Lewis to increase the pay and better working conditions of the coal miners. All the moral principles justifying and demanding collective bargaining in these cases apply with equal logic to the lay teachers in our schools."

If American Catholics in the future will give much more attention to promoting Catholic scholarship, it seems evident that the results will be greatly needed improvements in the general standing of all Catholics in comparison with other religious groups in our country, and in a better attitude toward Catholics by non-Catholics in secular education and, therefore, more Catholics will be more successful in securing positions in secular colleges and universities. This will not only prevent "abandoning the secular institutions to the secularists" but will also make the "atmosphere" of secular institutions much better for the majority of American Catholic youth in the impressionable years of their formal higher education.

The *Catholic World* [14] contains two fine articles for anyone interested in the problems of Catholic scholarship and Catholics in secular education. In the "Challenge of Secularism" Christopher Dawson has some very pointed remarks on this subject. "If we could develop Christian higher Education to a point at which it meets the attention of the average educated man in every field of thought and life, the situation would be radically changed." Granted that this is a high and wide objective, it is capable of being realized in a large part in the foreseeable future if Catholics in education,

[14] February, 1956. Published by the Paulist Fathers, 411 West 59th St., N. Y., N. Y.

both religious and secular, work consciously and conscientiously toward it in institutions of both kinds.
Dawson objects to what he calls "a kind of Catholic
Puritanism which separates itself as far as possible
from Secular culture and adopts an attitude of with-
drawal and intransigency." This attitude of with-
drawal, as has already been said in this book, is in a
large part responsible for the lack of reputation for
high scholarship on the part of many fine scholars on
the faculties of Catholic institutions who do not sufficiently exert themselves to participate in the scholarly
meetings and the scholarly publications of their general fields.

Gregory F. X. Delaunay,[15] in discussing the draw-
backs of teaching in Catholic colleges, mentions, of
course, the widespread lack of security, tenure, regular
increments, and relatively high salary. It seems to
many people who are obviously looking on from the
outside of these institutions that the lack of money is
not the whole explanation. Certainly more could be
done for security and tenure on present financial resources, if security and tenure were rated as highly by
the administrations of Catholic institutions as they
seem to be in most secular colleges and universities.

Perhaps Delaunay's most emphatic passages have to
do with the desirability of tremendously increasing the

[15] "Catholic Teachers at Secular Colleges," *ibid.*

number of really competent Catholic scholars and teachers in secular colleges and universities. "Indeed, on the secular campus he may by his very presence bring a leaven of Christian influence—perhaps the only one—into an otherwise materialistic milieu. To use his position for subtle proselytizing for the Church would, of course, be to betray his profession . . . but there is still much incidental good to be done, if only by way of providing sound answers to prevalent distortions of Catholic thought and history. In this he will undoubtedly work in close cooperation with the Newman Club." Again Delaunay remarks that the Catholic "teacher who lives his religion and at the same time commands their [the students'] intellectual respect offers living proof that all Catholics are not necessarily the regimented bigots that they may have been lead to believe. The sheer novelty of this example may exert greater influence than on a Catholic campus. . . ."

I doubt if the problem of academic freedom in a Catholic college is a serious handicap. No rational person ought to expect a Catholic, Protestant, or Jewish institution to pay a salary to anyone to teach doctrines fundamentally at variance with the doctrines the promotion of which is one of the great objectives of the institution. Probably a greater weakness is what Delaunay calls the " 'new broom' policies of each successive dean and president (who in most Catholic colleges are likely by the rules of their order to be changed every few years." Also it must be said that some of the criticisms of Catholic education are often legitimate criticisms of secular institutions. Weekly schedules of fifteen hours of teaching are not unknown in public colleges, and there are secular institutions in which no one outside of the offices of the presidents and the deans know what any teacher other than himself is being paid. Ideal conditions are not easily found in either secular or religious education, but if all of the educators in both systems *worked harmoniously together* both systems could be moved much closer to the ideal.

6

Released Time in Public Schools

The fact that one half of American Catholic children are in non-Catholic elementary schools, and 70 per cent of the Catholic youth who attend high school are in non-Catholic high schools—most of both groups doubtless in public schools—makes (or should make) the system of released time a matter of primary concern to all American Catholics.

The released time program is an agency for providing "weekday religious education sponsored by the churches for teaching children and youth who are excused from public school one or more periods a week upon the written request of their parents." [1] This program is primarily of concern to Protestants, though, I believe, most Catholics endorse it heartily, and in many communities Catholics utilize it and cooperate in its administration.

There are two types of released time operating in

[1] Leaflet from the Department of Weekday Religious Education, National Council of Churches of Christ, 79 East Adams St., Chicago 3, Ill.

the United States. Both are arrangements by which students in public schools are given religious instruction by various religious groups—Protestant, Catholic, Jewish, and so on—by teachers selected by, and of course supported by, any religious group which desires to use the system. The difference between the two types is that the older type taught the classes in the school buildings, in rooms that would otherwise be vacant at the hour at which the religious classes were taught. In the second type the students leave the school building and go to churches, synagogues, or some other building in which their group has arranged to hold the religious classes.

The *first* type, which is often spoken of as the Champaign type, or the Illinois type, was in operation in most of the states when the widely denounced Mc-Collum decision [1] of the United States Supreme Court in 1948 said that the system of having religious classes taught in public school buildings in school hours *constituted an establishment of religion,* and was, therefore, *unconstitutional under the First Amendment* which was *made applicable to the states by the Fourteenth Amendment.* As will be shown later, these three italicized statements of the Supreme Court violate the language and purpose of the First Amendment, the total history of its interpretation and application

[1] 303 U.S. 203 (1948), *op. cit.*

from 1791 to 1947, by Congress and the Presidency, and every relevant decision of the Supreme Court (both before and *after* the McCollum decision) in the entire history of the Court.

The *second* type of released time, frequently referred to as the New York type, came prominently to public notice in the Zorach [2] case in New York in 1952. In that case the religious classes were held outside the public school buildings. The only difference between the McCollum case and the Zorach case was that in the McCollum case the students used an otherwise empty room in a public school building in school hours, and in the Zorach case the students left the public school building, in school hours, to receive religious instruction elsewhere.

The point of the *use* of the building, the expense involved in the wear and tear, for instance, on the floors of the rooms in which the students were being taught religion (instead of the wear and tear on the floors in the rooms in which they would have been if they had not been in these rooms) is clearly too silly to be seriously considered by mature people. The United States Supreme Court, in the McCollum case, gave no serious consideration to that point, nor was it argued in the briefs or by the attorneys on either side of the McCollum case. In other words, it was a point that

[2] *Op. cit.*

was not so much as mentioned except in one passage in which Justice Jackson dismissed the public expense of the practice at Champaign, Illinois, as of no importance.

In a pamphlet entitled *Weekday Religious Education at the High School Level*,[3] Lois V. McClure writes, "Most of the classes in the 121 communities [reporting on a certain questionnaire] giving information about where the classes are held reported the use of public school buildings, despite the opinion rendered in the Champaign, Illinois, case in 1948 by the United States Supreme Court outlawing their use for the program in that community."

Attorney General Latham Castle of Illinois has ruled, according to a newsstory from Chicago,[4] that religious instruction classes may be conducted on Illinois public school premises before or after regular school hours providing the attendance at the classes is voluntary, that in the McCollum case the Supreme Court prohibited the conduct of released time religious instruction in the public school buildings during regular school hours. The Attorney General of the State of Oregon, Robert Y. Thornton, reported [5] that a 1925 State law

[3] Reprinted from *Religious Education*, January-February, 1952, published by the National Council of Churches of Christ in the U.S.A., 79 East Adams St., Chicago 3, Ill., p. 16. This article is a digest of a thesis for the Master of Arts degree at Northwestern University.

[4] *The Catholic Transcript* (Hartford), March 31, 1955.

[5] *The Tablet* (Brooklyn, N.Y.), January 8, 1955.

providing that children may attend released time instruction classes is still valid. The Oregon law states that when parents or guardians request that children be excused to attend such classes the school boards may release them providing that classes do not total more than two hours a week and do not interfere with regular school activities. Whether other state attorneys have made the same ruling and, if so, how many of them I have no way of knowing, but it seems quite evident that these rulings put an end to any serious argument that the McCollum decision necessarily prohibits the use of public property for religious education. Obviously, in the light of American history, it would be strange to have a situation in which public property could be used to promote almost any conceivable idea except the idea of religion, but that would not be much stranger than the thought that public education cannot cooperate with religion, since all state governments and the federal government have always cooperated with religion throughout our history. This leaves, in the McCollum decision, only the very narrow doctrine that the public education authorities are the only public authorities that are prohibited from having any impartial cooperative contact with religious movements. Religion is thus substantially the only interest of the American people that could be publicly approved by millions and yet be the only one from which public education must be prevented from having any mutually advantageous contacts.

Dr. Irwin L. Shaver, executive director of the Department of Weekday Religious Education, reports [6] that according to the information which he has at the present time he estimates that there are, in the released time classes in the United States, about 1,750,000 Protestant children and about one million Catholic children. There are relatively few Jewish children enrolled, most of them in New York City. The best estimate is about eight thousand children of the Jewish faith in these classes. Dr. Walter Howlett, director of the released time classes for the Catholics, Protestants and Jews in New York City, estimates [7] that released time classes are being conducted in three thousand communities in the United States and that there are about three million enrolled in the classes.

The scheme is apparently very widespread, particularly in the cities of the country. The number of Catholics enrolled in the released time classes in the various communities is not obtainable; the most reliable estimates I have found indicate that the number runs to around 30,000 in some of the largest cities.

[6] Letter to J. M. O'Neill, October 14, 1955,
[7] Letter to J. M. O'Neill, August 31, 1955.

Certainly one of the most illuminating volumes concerning religion in education in our country at the present time is *American Education and Religion,* subtitled "The Problem of Religion in the Schools." [8] This book is based on a series of lectures given at the Institute of Religious and Social Studies of the Jewish Theological Seminary of America in the winter of 1950–1951.

Dr. Johnson gave the opening statement and the summaries and conclusions at the end of the volume. In addition, ten well-known spokesmen for various religions and various educational institutions each presented his own personal view in regard to the problem. It is a fine contribution to current discussions in regard to religion. A Jewish educator's view was presented by Dr. Simon Greenberg, vice-chancellor and Professor of Homiletics in the Jewish Theological Seminary of America. A Catholic educator's view was presented by Right Reverend Monsignor Frederick G. Hochwalt, director of the Department of Education, National Catholic Welfare Conference. A Protestant educator's view was presented by Dr. Nevin C. Harner, Professor of Christian Education, Theological Seminary of the Evangelical and Reformed Church.

The only major flaw in the volume, in my opinion, is

[8] Edited by Ernest F. Johnson, published by the Institute of Religious and Social Studies, distributed by Harper & Bros., New York, 1952.

the almost constant use of the ambiguous phrase "the separation of church and state" for the meaning of the very specific establishment clause of the First Amendment which means, and always has meant to those who have followed the thinking of Madison and Jefferson, *an exclusive position of governmental favor granted by the government to one religious group.*

The best statements concerning the meaning of the Establishment clause are "Religion in a State University," by Dr. J. Hillis Miller, president of the University of Florida. He discusses this problem principally on pages 104 and 105 where he says, "We believe that our forefathers' concern for the equality of religious sects should not be construed as 'the separation of church and state.'" It was considered in those early days, and should be so construed now, as the guarantee for the political equality for all religious groups. This is, beyond any question, the only interpretation of the Establishment clause that can be found expressed, or held to be consistent with, the writings or official actions of either Jefferson or Madison, or of the other founding fathers and people of that day. However, the ambiguous phrase is widely used throughout the volume and given various erroneous specific interpretations. On page 51 a statement is made about "the absolute separation of church and state in a Jeffersonian version."

Dr. Harner, in stating the basic principles of Protestantism, mentioned (p. 83) "a firm adherence to the principle of the separation of church and state," but he immediately expressed what this meant to him by quoting the remark of the American Council on Education's Committee on Religion and Education, as follows: "The core of meaning in the doctrine of separation of church and state we believe to be this: There shall be no ecclesiastical control of political functions; there shall be no political dictation in the eccesiastical sphere except as public safety or public morals may require it." This "core of meaning" remark is clearly the result of not having any exclusive favor granted to any church, or no union between the church and the government as is the case in countries which have established churches, such as Spain, Sweden, and other European countries.

In his excellent statement of the problem, Dr. Johnson says [9] (pp. 12–13), "a feeling of amazed frustration at the decision of the Supreme Court in the McCollum case which, temporarily at least, threw the released time plan into confusion. Here was a plan laboriously worked out, mainly under Protestant auspices but with active Catholic support and participation, developed through many years of experimentation, and specifically designed to preserve the separation of church and

[9] See footnote 7 of this chapter.

state as Protestants, its historic champions, understood the doctrine. Even assuming that the decision was just and wise—and there is wide disagreement on the point —it should occasion no wonder that Protestant leaders were dismayed by it and impelled to develop a more positive strategy." Dr. Johnson doubtless means the American type of separation just discussed, which has had the support of Protestants, Catholics, and Jews throughout our history, and is today supported by substantially all Americans.

In another passage, page 9, Dr. Johnson writes, "It is not strange that in the light of recent developments there should be an increase in the number of religious day schools." That there has been an increase in the number of religious day schools and that other speakers on this program remarked on the rapid growth of such schools in recent years is undoubtedly largely due to the activity of the Supreme Court in trying to be, as Professor Corwin of Princeton remarked, "a super board of education for all the United States."

Dr. Vivian Thayer, formerly educational director of the Ethical Culture Schools, in an essay entitled *An Experimentalist Position*, expressed essentially the point of view of the secularist in education. Dr. Thayer objects to the statement on secularism by the Catholic bishops of America, following a conference in November, 1949, and to the statement about secularism in the pamphlet *The Relation of Religion to Public Education* issued by the committee of the American Council of Education in 1947. He opposes remarks about secularism which "ascribe a sectarian purpose to a movement that has as its primary objective the emancipation of men from the limitations of sectarianism." On page 31 Dr. Thayer speaks of secularism as follows: "Here is a faith that conflicts with the tenets of traditional religion. But, in all fairness, we should recognize it for what it is; an affirmation of faith, a religion, if you will, which entitled it to the right of competition in the market place with all of the privileges and of the limitations that apply to the propagation of other religions."

Dr. Johnson's comment on the above, on page 197, is: "Now it seems to me that Dr. Thayer has here described not what is 'secular' but what is *public*, and hence inclusive and must be under secular direction in order to be non-sectarian. But *secularism* is a term with a history and I think it must be defined in relation to its history. It is widely used to denote, not the secular areas of life, but a way of living and thinking that makes the secular self sufficient and renders religion irrelevant. If secularism connoted nothing but the secular areas of life, there would be no argument over it."

Further on, on page 33, Dr. Thayer writes: "Secularism is thus a way of thinking which seeks to promote mutual understanding and good will in a realm where, as Justice Frankfurter has said, conflicts are most easily and bitterly engendered. . . . It is a logic and a discipline by means of which men seek to raise themselves above the battle of religious sects."

A timely observation by Dr. Greenberg has direct relevance to a matter discussed in the paragraph on the pamphlet *Public Education and the Future of America.* In discussing a possible "law compelling all children to spend at least a part of their student days in public schools," Dr. Greenberg wrote: "It would, of course, be a sad day for America if such an issue were ever to become subject to widespread public discussion directed toward definite political action. The very rise of the issue would indicate a serious deterioration in our social structure." (Pp. 49–50)

Dr. Thayer's position in regard to secularism is consistent with a number of other explanations of secularism which are common in the literature, namely, an explanation which claims, in one set of circumstances that secularism is a religion entitled to all the privileges of any religion, and in another set of circumstances, that secularism is not a religion; it is the opposite of religion, and, therefore, it is not to be banned from the schools when religion is banned from the schools. This, of course, gives to secularism the advantage of having privileges in the market place which no other attitude in the whole field of religious thinking—pro or con—is entitled to under the edict of the Supreme Court.

Dr. F. Ernest Johnson, writing in *Current Religious Thought*,[10] has what is probably one of the most complete and analytical discussions of religion in education to be found in any article of similar length. His basic position is "either the whole of life will become secularized because religion is given no place in the education system that furnishes the youth with patterns of thought and conduct *or* religion will come to be recognized as a vital factor in the common culture and as such studied in the schools. . . . Many Protestant scholars have begun to ask whether the public school will not be maintained at too high a price if the inevitable result is a complacent indifference to religion. . . . I am not advocating that the school 'teach' religion as a church is free to teach it. Quite the contrary . . . what I am here pleading for is a frank facing of the problem. The most distressing aspect of this situation is that many Christian ministers and laymen—some of the latter public school teachers and administrators —see nothing anomalous in the attempt to build around a program of education, one which includes the whole range of human interest, with religion as the one conspicuous exception."

[10] (Oberlin, Ohio), February, 1950, pp. 23–28. Quoted with permission.

Dr. Johnson speaks of the religious community in America being "rudely shocked by pronouncements of the Supreme Court. I am satisfied that this new Protestant demand [that is, for the introduction of teaching religion objectively, or teaching about religion in the public schools] would never have been heard had not Protestant leaders been startled by what seemed to be a progressive crowding out of everything connected with religion from the program of general education made accessible to the children and youth. I think the proposal that the school should indoctrinate with a basic metaphysics is unsound but it arose as a natural protest and it will have to be reckoned with. . . .

"Frankly, no one knows now what will stand the Supreme Court test in this area. If the ruling opinions in the Everson and McCollum cases are applied with literal exactness, then a revolution in present and traditional practice will follow. Literally, the doctrine that the state may not 'aid religion, aid all religions, or prefer one religion over another' might well be taken to end the chaplaincy in the armed forces and in penal institutions, free lunches to parochial school children, all addresses on religion, such as the President made recently, and many other things to which the nation has become accustomed. I think, however, it is highly unlikely that the Supreme Court, in further clarifying its position as it will be obliged to do, will condemn every recognition in the program of public education of religion as a concern of human beings."

That leading Protestant spokesmen are as much opposed to the McCollum decision as Catholic spokesmen are is further illustrated by an address before the Board of Education and the National Association of Schools and Colleges of the Methodist Church by Dr. Edward McCready, president of The University of the South, at Sewanee, Tennessee. According to a newsstory from Cincinnati,[11] Dr. McCready, an Episcopalian, in addressing a group of Methodist educators spoke in part, as follows: "The decision . . . has, on casual reading, a pious sound, but I am not so sure that I am able to comprehend what kind of freedom of belief it is which this ruling purports to preserve.

"I think that everyone should be free to believe that the world is flat, if he can find that credible; but this does not mean that the Supreme Court should protect any such believers from the embarrassment of hearing that there are intelligent people who think it approximately spherical.

"I ask no more for religion than I do for geography in the educational process, but I also ask for no less."

The system of released time in the public schools of the United States, properly administered, would offer one of the best possible agencies for assisting pastors

[11] *The Pilot* (Boston), January 22, 1955.

and parents in attending to the religious needs of many of the millions of Catholic children in the public schools of the United States.

If this system is to be easily and competently administered, and to operate without wholly unnecessary inconvenience to the parents who wish to make use of it, the great obstacle to such desirable functioning, the McCollum decision of the United States Supreme Court in 1948, must be gotten out of the way.

Even though, since the Zorach (see below) decision in 1952, the McCollum decision is no longer an effective block to religious education, it is still a serious obstacle which makes much more difficult the proper exercise of freedom of religion and freedom of education.

Released time is expanding rapidly in accord with the Zorach decision, and in many places it is operating just as it did in Champaign, Illinois, under the theory which many people accept and apply, i.e., that the local schools of any community are in control of the people of that community according to American tradition and constitutions, and are not to be administered by the Supreme Court of the United States.

In certain journals and books an attempt is made to spread the idea that the opposition to the decision in the McCollum case is a *Catholic attack* on the Supreme Court, and that Protestants and other Americans defend the Supreme Court in the McCollum decision, thus producing a *Catholic versus Protestant* controversy about the meaning of the religious clause of the First Amendment. The *Christian Century* [12] misses few, if any, opportunities to promote this idea. Among the books which make the same attempt are Paul Blanshard's *American Freedom and Catholic Power*; [13] Conrad H. Moehlman's *The Wall of Separation Between Church and State*; [14] Leo Pfeffer's *Church, State, and Freedom*,[15] and Joseph Martin Dawson's *America's Way in Church, State, and Society*.[16] This idea that there is a Catholic-Protestant controversy on the validity of the McCollum decision is simply an invention for propaganda purposes beamed at the uninformed. Protestant ministers are the principal promoters and administrators of released time throughout the country —as they were the principal supports of the Board of Education in Champaign in opposition to Mrs. McCollum.

It is difficult to understand how any literate person who is actually interested in the relation of government to religion in the United States could avoid knowing most of the following facts, *all of which* deny that the

[12] 407 South Dearborn St., Chicago 5, Ill.
[13] (Boston: Beacon Press, 1949.)
[14] (Boston: Beacon Press, 1951.)
[15] (Boston: Beacon Press, 1953.)
[16] (New York: Macmillan, 1953.)

Catholics have a monopoly in condemning the Mc-Collum decision.

A group of twenty-five distinguished Protestant ministers and educators, in June, 1948, protested against the "interpretation that has been formulated by the Supreme Court" and affirmed the "interpretation of the American doctrine of separation of Church and State" as "cooperation entered into freely by the State and Church and involving no special privilege to any Church and no threat to the religious liberty of any citizen." Six months later the Catholic bishops, after their annual meeting in Washington, issued an official statement in which they took substantially the same position in almost identical words: "We feel with deep conviction that for the sake of both good citizenship and religion there should be a reaffirmation of our original American tradition of free cooperation between government and religious bodies—cooperation involving no special privilege to any group and no restriction on the religious liberty of any citizen."

Leading Protestant historians and scholars in constitutional law; the *American Bar Association Journal*; the record of every president of the United States—Washington to Eisenhower both included, as well as both Jefferson and Madison; every Congress in our history; the record, the current practice of every state in the Union, and every relevant Supreme Court decision in the history of the Court, are all in agreement with some Catholics in opposition to the Supreme Court in its lonely McCollum decision. The Catholic Church, of course, takes no position on the meaning of a phrase in the Constitution. The proof of all this is widely available. Ample references to all of it, accurately documented, can be found in two books published since the McCollum decision.[17]

In any realistic discussion of the future of American education, secular or religious, and particularly a discussion of the relation of religion to public education (which is much the largest part of our secular education area), it seems necessary to say something about a problem which is confusing, and in many instances delaying the solution of many important questions in American education. That is the problem of the relation of government to religion, or "Church and State." This relationship bears on the question of the authority of government over public education. Obviously any legal exercise of government control over education must be in accordance with the Constitution of the United States and the constitution of the individual state concerned in any particular instance of such control. States vary necessarily in their constitutions and laws, and the legislatures and the courts of the states

---

[17] J. M. O'Neill, *Religion and Education under the Constitution* (New York: Harpers & Bros., 1949), chaps. V–IX; and *Catholicism and American Freedom,* chap. IV, pp. 55–58.

should be allowed to carry out the will of the people of the states in education as in other areas—unless it can be shown that there has been a failure to observe the mandates of the Federal Constitution as ratified by the people of the states. Whether or not the state action agrees with what the justices of the Supreme Court think is wise and good for the people of a state from which an appeal comes is irrelevant.

Most of the confusion arises from the fact that the Supreme Court justices and many other commentators, instead of using the clear language of the First Amendment: "Congress shall make no law respecting an establishment of religion," use the ambiguous phrase "the complete separation of Church and State" (which is in no constitution in America) as a fog under which all sorts of meanings can be exploited. In the McCollum case the Court followed Justice Rutledge in a dissenting opinion in the Everson bus case of the year before which was that the purpose of the First Amendment was "a complete and permanent separation of the spheres of religious activity and civil authority by comprehensively forbidding every form of public aid or support to religion. The prohibition broadly forbids State support, financial or other, of religion in any guise, form or degree. It outlaws all use of public funds for religious purposes."

The two most important court cases involving released time are the McCollum case [18] and the Zorach case.[19] The former case came up from Champaign, Illinois, where released time was operating at the request of the parents of a large group of children, in the public school buildings in school hours. This activity was conducted in accordance with the laws of the state, with the approval of the State Department of Education, the local school board, and was upheld by the Supreme Court of the state.

The mother of one child, Mrs. McCollum, started legal action to stop the program as a violation of the Establishment clause of the First Amendment. Her little boy was not in the program, since she had not requested that he be allowed to register; but she objected to the others doing what she would not allow her child to do. At the time when she began her action there were, in the program in Champaign, Protestant, Catholic, and Jewish children, in decreasing numbers in that order.

In the decision of the United States Supreme Court it was proclaimed, without any serious attempt at explanation or argument, that the program objected to constituted "an establishment of religion" and so was unconstitutional under the First Amendment as transferred to the states by the Fourteenth. The justices

[18] 333 U.S. 203 (1948), *op. cit.*
[19] 343 U.S. 306 (1952).

claimed that their decision was in agreement with the *purpose* of the First Amendment, and the positions of Jefferson and Madison, none of which was, or could be, substantiated. Anyone who reads the justices' opinions in this case could hardly escape noting the appalling lack of any legitimate grounds for this decision.

The heart of the case of *Zorach* v. *Clauson* [20] was given by Mr. Justice Douglas speaking for the Court, as follows:

This released time program involves neither religious instruction in public school classrooms nor the expenditure of public funds. All costs, including the application blanks, are paid by the religious organizations. The case is, therefore, unlike McCollum versus Board of Education . . . in that case the classrooms were turned over to religious instructors. We accordingly held that the program violated the First Amendment which (by reason of the Fourteenth Amendment) prohibits the states from establishing religion or prohibiting its free exercise.

It takes obtuse reasoning to inject any issue of the "free exercise" of religion into the present case. No one is forced to go to the religious classroom and no religious exercise or instruction is brought to the classrooms of the public schools. . . . We do not see how New York by this type of released time program has made a law respecting an establishment of religion within the meaning of the First Amendment.

[20] *Ibid.*

Justice Douglas, in the Zorach opinion, had the tough job of trying to reconcile the irreconcilable—the Court's McCollum decision that allowing children in a public school to go to otherwise vacant rooms for religious education in school hours *is an establishment of religion*, but that the Zorach decision in allowing pupils to go off the school premises for religious education in school hours *is not an establishment of religion*. Both plans required the cooperation of the public school system; both excused pupils from school work in some school hours at the request of the pupil's parents, and neither gave a favored position or special privilege to any religion.

Here is the attempt of the Justice to execute his assignment:

There cannot be the slightest doubt that the First Amendment reflects the philosophy that Church and State should be separated, and so far as interference with the free exercise of religion and an establishment of religion are concerned, the separation must be complete and unequivocable. The First Amendment within the scope of its coverage permits no exception, the prohibition is absolute. The First Amendment, however, does not say that in every and all respects there shall be a separation of Church and State. Rather it studiously defines the manner, the specific way in which there shall be no concert or union or dependency one upon the other.

Perhaps the First Amendment *reflects* the above philosophy; it does not express it. The First Amendment *records the fact* that Congress may not legislate concerning "an establishment of religion." In doing this the First Amendment makes clear to future generations that Congress has been given *no power to establish a national religion,* and that, of course, is a type of separation of Church and State. No monopolistic favor granted to one religious group by the government is the American type of separation of Church and State. It differs, incidentally, from the type of separation of Church and State in all other countries. But neither the Constitution of the United States nor that of any state in the union uses the words "separation of Church and State" in any connection with the relations of Church and State or of government and religion.

Since public funds were not involved in either McCollum or Zorach, and since neither raised an issue of religious freedom, the one and only point of difference between the two cases is that, in McCollum, classrooms were used in school hours, and in Zorach the children went off the school premises for the religious education. This leaves only one possible theory which could justify the McCollum decision and require the Court to attempt to reconcile it with the Zorach decision—a theory which no justice of the Court has ever been reckless enough to try to explain or justify to the American bar, the political scientists, and other Americans who are interested in our American freedoms and in some self government in the states. This theory is clearly that any cooperation (even one without expense and desired by the overwhelming majority of the population of a district) between the local schools and the local religious organizations is prohibited by the First Amendment. Anyone who knows the constitutional and social history of the United States knows that this fantastic theory violates the language and purpose of both the First Amendment and the Fourteenth Amendment and the interpretation and application of the First Amendment since 1791, and of the Fourteenth Amendment since 1868, by the Congress, the Presidency, and the Supreme Court.

The nearest Justice Black came to giving reasons for the opinion of the Court in the McCollum case was as follows: "Here not only are the state's tax-supported public school buildings used for the dissemination of religious doctrines. The state also affords sectarian groups invaluable aid in that it helps to provide pupils for their religious classes through use of the state's compulsory public school machinery. This is not separation of Church and State." [21]

Whether any particular practice is "separation of Church and State" depends on what is meant by this

[21] The official Court report citation. 333 U.S. 203 (1948), 212.

superlatively ambiguous phrase, and any consideration
of which of its many possible meanings properly applies to any problem of constitutional interpretation
is wholly irrelevant anyway since this language does
not appear in the Constitution of the United States nor
in the constitution of any American state. Every state
helps "sectarian groups" by providing "pupils for their
religious classes through the use of the state's compulsory school machinery"—*not* the state's "compulsory
public school machinery," as Justice Black remarked.
No state has such machinery; school attendance laws
apply equally to public and private, secular and religious schools. No state compels children to attend
secular schools. The states of the United States in their
compusory school attendance laws simply compel children to go to school—to whatever school the parents of
the children select for their attendance. Any school
which meets the ordinary standards of the educational
laws of the state comes under the compulsory school
attendance laws. And once a child is registered in a
religious school of any denomination the state authority compels him to attend.

Justice Black should have known that no state has
compulsory public school machinery or ever has had
since Oregon attempted it in 1922, and the Supreme

Court, in 1925, unanimously ruled that the Oregon law making such an attempt was unconstitutional.[22] It seems probable that Justice Black learned that the states did not have compulsory public school machinery after his decision was published, because in some later reports of this opinion, as, for instance, in the quotation which he used in the Zorach dissent (p. 4289) from his opinion in the McCollum case, he omitted the word "public" and spoke only of the "State's compulsory school machinery." But on the same page he speaks of the state's "power to compel children to attend secular schools." Justice Black should investigate the various state school attendance laws, and Supreme Court decisions regarding them, before discussing them further in his Supreme Court opinions.

In the same paragraph he complains that "New York is manipulating its compulsory education laws to help religious sects get pupils." Every state in the United States which has compulsory education laws helps religious sects get pupils in their religious schools and always has.

Justice Black assumes, in his opinions in both the McCollum and the Zorach cases, that the First Amendment is a constitutional mandate to keep church and

[22] Pierce v. Society of Sisters, 268 U.S. 510 (1925).

state completely separate and that, therefore, a state
can no more aid all religions impartially than it can aid
one. If Justice Black is accurate in this he must necessarily believe (if he is acquainted with American history) that the United States government from 1791,
and every state in the union from 1868, has been in-
dulging in countless unconstitutional actions and all
are doing it today. And no one discovered it until
1947.

Justice Black also has a strange footnote [23] in which
he says that a state policy for aiding all religions necessarily requires a governmental decision as to what constitutes "a religion. Thus is created a governmental
power to hinder certain religious beliefs by denying
their character to be such. . . . This provides precisely
the kind of censorship [sic] which we have said the
Constitution forbids." Such a decision, even if an out-
rageously improper one under the relevant statutes,
would not be *censorship;* furthermore, the Supreme
Court has to decide what constitutes religion every
time it decides a "freedom of religion" case. The Court
has acted on such religion cases many times. Also, the
Constitution contains nothing that says a Supreme
Court justice may not know even what the word "religion" means. In fact, in one case the Court phrased

[23] *United States Law Week* (Washington, D.C.), April 29, 1952, p.
4289, note 4.

a definition which is substantially in accord with the definition of the lexicographers, the Catholic Church, Jefferson, Madison, and the usual use by Protestants, Jews, and others who use language competently. Justice Field, speaking for the Court,[24] said, "The term religion has reference to one's views of his relation to his Creator, and to the obligations they impose of reverence for His being and character, and of obedience to his will." [25]

If the general power of Congress to aid religion, impartially of course, must be denied because under it some agency of the government might make a mistake, why should not the power of Congress to aid education, agriculture, commerce, or aviation be denied for the same reason?

In the McCollum case in which Justice Black was the spokesman for the Court, the decision was clearly not only based on some assumed definition of "religion," but on an assumption of the meaning of *an establishment of religion* which has been generally held to be a false assumption by informed critics of that unique decision. That decision "hindered certain religious beliefs" by denying to all positive religious groups privileges granted to secularists, agnostics, and atheists. In fact, it substantially gave a combination

[24] Reynolds v. United States, 98 U.S. 145 (1879).
[25] O'Neill, *Religion and Education under the Constitution*, pp. 5–7.

of these three groups some of the privileges of an "established religion" of the United States.

When the Zorach case came before the Supreme Court, the justices were doubtless aware of the tremendous opposition to the McCollum decision in all sections of the population.

Professor Pritchett, of the University of Chicago, writing of the opinion of the Court in the Zorach case —Justice Douglas speaking for the Court—said: "The McCollum decision raised a furore in church circles, for similar released time programs were in effect throughout the country. As Black himself later admitted: 'Probably few opinions from this Court in recent years have attracted more attention or stirred wider debate . . .'

"The weaknesses of the Douglas position suggests that the Court majority was disposed to use any available method to quiet the storm caused by the McCollum decision. This impression seems to be strengthened by the position the Court took in the New Jersey Bible Reading Case, Doremus v. the Board of Education,[27] decided a month prior to Zorach v. Clauson. Here the Court avoided making any decision at all on the constitutionality of the state statute providing for the reading without comment of five verses of the Old Testament at the opening of each public school day.

[27] 342 U.S. 429 (1952).

Its grounds were technical ones of lack of standing on the part of the plaintiff to maintain the suit. This theory of avoiding trouble, however, runs afoul of the fact that Justices Douglas, Reed and Burton, who composed half the Zorach majority, dissented in Doremus." [26]

Inconsistency with decisions immediate both in time and in relevancy seems not to trouble the Supreme Court. The only *possible* constitutional validity of the McCollum decision (that the Fourteenth Amendment applied the Bill of Rights *per se* to the states) was denied just before the McCollum case came up, in Adamson v. California,[28] and just after, in Wolf v. Colorado.[29] Neither the McCollum nor the Zorach case was a "religious freedom" case, but "an establishment of religion" case, and the Supreme Court has held again and again that the Fourteenth Amendment protects only the great fundamental personal freedoms *implicit in a scheme of ordered liberty from state violation* in its words "liberty without due process of law," and does not make the whole Bill of Rights a limitation on state power—or, as Justice Frankfurter has vividly expressed it, a "shorthand summary of the first eight Amendments." However, a federal prohibition of "an

---

[26] C. Herman Pritchett, *Civil Liberties and the Vinson Court* (Chicago: University of Chicago Press, 1954), pp. 12, 14.

[28] 312 U.S. 46 (1947).

[29] 338 U.S. 25 (1949).

establishment of religion" is rather futile anyway since the constitutions of all the states forbid it, and no American of any creed or party is apparently in favor of one. If the Court has been right in its position whenever the question has been formally before it for determination, then the phrase "an establishment of religion" has no channel by which it can be transferred to the states from Congress. The careless and casual phrases to the contrary (never once explained or defended by any justice) are only *dicta* to bolster up the proclaiming of private opinions as to what is good for the people of the several states.

I suppose that all somewhat educated Americans know that religion is one, probably the chief, of the civilizing influences in human history, which is the background of American life. If the free people of a sovereign state wish to use their own school buildings fairly and competently (within the state constitutions and laws and the regulations of the educational authorities, state and local) to help enlighten young Americans concerning this most important subject, the theory that the states have tied the hands of every state to prevent it from exercising this instance of self-government is both absurd and incapable of proof.

7

Newman Clubs and Catholic Student Centers

I recently spent a week end on the campus of a large secular men's college, in which there is a strong and active Newman Club, housed in a handsome Catholic student center, and directed by an enthusiastic and devoted chaplain. On Sunday morning I saw 227 Catholic college men receive Holy Communion at Mass in the neighboring church. The bishop of the diocese came that day to speak at the Communion breakfast and in the afternoon to confirm nine recently converted college students. Two of the nine were Phi Beta Kappa's of the senior class, and one of these is now in a seminary starting his preparation for the priesthood. I once heard a Newman Club chaplain say that the one strongest influence responsible for conversions among college students is the Catholic roommate.

If all counselors and advisers of the Catholic youth who are about to enter non-Catholic education would "accentuate the positive" and imbue the students with the idea that they are going into a situation in which they would have some fine opportunities to make *their influence* count on the side of good conduct and the spread of accurate information about the Church and American Catholics (when information is called for), the dangers in secular education would be greatly diminished. This seems obviously a better program than one which assumes that the student is a weak character and, in going into a secular college, is in great danger of surrendering to the *influence of others* and so acquiring subversive or immoral traits, or of leaving the Church altogether.

Every informed person knows that there are some dangers to faith and morals in secular education, especially for students whose intellectual, religious, and moral life has not been sufficiently developed to make it safe for them to leave home to "go out into the world" for either work or study.

Dr. Raymond J. Sontag, professor of European history at the University of California at Berkeley, writing in *Thought*[1] concerning the Catholic undergraduates in non-Catholic institutions of higher learning, says: "Too few of these have either the knowledge or the mature judgment to live spiritually without the support of family and parish, with only such support as can be given by the relatively few Catholic profes-

[1] (New York), March, 1949, p. 30.

sors and students, and by the Catholic chaplain if there be one. This is a fact which should be squarely faced by parents . . . by the sisters and priests, already over-worked, who are responsible for the religious educa-tion of the young." If the Catholic press was well in-formed in the early autumn of 1955, there is little hope of changing the already reported situation (see Chapter 2) to one where most Catholic youth would be able to go to Catholic high schools and colleges. It follows that not only the parents, but all who have any responsibility for the education of the young (and even those who have no direct responsibility, but who are interested in the future) should face the situation, and try to provide what is apparently the only remedy—to change the situation on the secular campuses by providing more, many more Catholic chaplains at once, and then to adopt a long-term plan to prepare more young Catho-lics for teaching and research in secular education. Badly prepared Catholics (and apparently even some very well-prepared Catholics) run into danger and sometimes succumb wherever they are. Some young Catholics in secular colleges, some who never go to any college, and even some who go to Catholic colleges, develop bad habits and even leave the Church.

The position that in our country, now or in the fore-seeable future, Catholics should keep out of secular education is neither realistic nor helpful. First, it would

surrender the whole field of public education to the
non-Catholic groups, and go far toward making a fact
out of the already too prevalent assumption that the
public system of education is a Protestant system which
is being rapidly transformed into a secularist, agnostic,
atheistic system. And it would mean the majority of
American Catholics would have no opportunity to get
any formal education beyond the elementary grades.
Catholics who are interested in the future of America
should be deeply concerned about whether the public
schools promote the ideals, and offer the kind and
quality of education which they believe in, and should
never lose sight of the fact that the public schools, colleges, and universities of any district, city, or state belong to the Catholics in every respect, in the same way
and on the same terms that apply to any other groups
in the community.

Clearly the majority of the Catholic students in secular higher education are in public institutions. It
seems evident that the great body of American Catholics must do much more than has ever been done to
improve the chances of these Catholic students of getting the good and avoiding the bad in secular education. Again it seems evident (at least to all the Catholics experienced in secular education whose opinions I
have heard or read) that the best and probably the
only way to do this is to provide more, and better sup-

ported, Newman clubs or Catholic student centers throughout the country.

There are more than six hundred Newman clubs and Catholic student centers with chaplains serving them in these institutions. All of the state universities have Newman clubs, and 116 public colleges as well. There is apparently available no complete listing of the private and religious non-Catholic institutions at which there are Newman clubs, but a rather extensive sampling of such institutions will illustrate something of the spread of the Newman Club program. These include Harvard, Boston University, Massachusetts Institute of Technology, Yale, Princeton, New York University, Columbia, Johns Hopkins, Western Reserve, Cornell, Chicago, Northwestern, Stanford, and University of Southern California. In addition to the state universities mentioned above there are a large number of public, tax-supported, municipal colleges such as those in Detroit and the four in New York City, the Naval Academy at Annapolis and the Military Academy at West Point. Clubs have been formed also at the very large number of private institutions of the college grade, to mention a few of the oldest, including Bowdoin, Tufts, Wellesley, Radcliffe, Vassar, Smith, Brown, Dartmouth, Amherst, and Williams.

The organization and programs of the different Newman clubs vary considerably from one institution to another. A number of them give regular courses for credit with members of the faculty regularly appointed by the officers of the institution, and in some with the administrative costs of the religious courses carried by the institution. The salaries, however, are usually paid by the particular church or religious organization which furnishes the teachers.

Probably the most elaborate organization is that at the State University of Iowa, in Iowa City. Here there are nine courses in religion offered by the Catholic chaplain who is a member of the faculty of the University. These courses are offered for credit in the regular university curriculum in the School of Religion in the university, whose faculty consists of two Protestant ministers, one Catholic priest, and one Jewish rabbi. A student of the university may freely elect the courses, may major in the department, and earn a master's degree, or a Ph.D. with a major interest in religion.

This program in a great tax-supported state university is at the present time doubtless the best and most thoroughly organized program in religious education in any public institution. It has been functioning on this basis for a number of years and is doubtless closer to the ideal of religious-minded Americans than any other such program to be found in a public institution in the United States.

Other examples of the status of courses given by the

chaplains show various situations. In the University of Illinois two priests offer ten courses for credit to any student who is a sophomore or above in the university. The university committee passes on the qualifications of the teachers and the courses as they would for any members of the faculty or courses in the university.

At the University of North Dakota there is an interesting situation which is expressed as follows: "The university, after stating its recognition of the Newman Foundation as an educational institution of the Catholic Church in North Dakota, expressed the general principle of its relation to the Churches: 'The university is supported by taxation of all the citizens of the State, and most of these citizens are members of some religious organization. Therefore, it is considered proper that the Churches of the State should have the privilege of using the facilities afforded by the University in the conduct of their educational work. The University has the obligation of training the youth of the State for their civil duties as citizens. The function of the Church is to educate the youth in sound morals and to accomplish this must maintain schools to insure competent instruction in religious and denominational work. *There is no conflict between the work of these institutions. It is wise economy for these agencies to use the facilities and advantages of each other in the conduct of their work, maintaining a strict separation as regards control and expenditure of the financial resources of each.'* " [2] (Italics added.)

In New York University, a private institution with over 9,000 Catholic students, about one fourth of the total enrollment, a Catholic chaplain, appointed as assistant professor on the faculty of the university, gives two courses of three credits each in the university curriculum. At Bradley University (private), in Peoria, Illinois, three priests attached to local parishes teach in the university, giving courses in religion up to a maximum of twelve credits. The courses are given in the university building. The priests (one of whom is the chaplain director and the other two his assistants) are appointed as assistant professors on the Bradley faculty.

The public Michigan State College at East Lansing, Michigan, has a department of religion which, to quote the college catalog, was established on the principle that "religion is an integral part of culture, and even in a public institution, a proper field of knowledge." The department of religion includes four Protestant ministers, a Catholic priest, and a Jewish rabbi, as well as two laymen. All courses carry academic credit, and a minor for the doctor's degree may be taken in the department of religion. There are three Catholic courses

[2] "The Newman Club in American Education," a pamphlet, published by the National Association of Newman Club Chaplains (Washington, D.C., 1953), p. 15.

taught by the Newman Club chaplain (pastor of the campus parish) and his one assistant. The Newman Club publication says that more Catholic students could be served if more priests were available. An administrative ruling of the college limits the number of students per section to fifty.

In Columbia University two courses in Catholic theology taught by priests are offered for three credits each. Noncredit courses in Catholic philosophy and religion are offered at Louisiana State University, the University of California, the University of Pennsylvania, Cornell University, Vanderbilt University, Wayne University in Detroit, and the Inter-Collegiate Newman Club in Cleveland, which includes Western Reserve University, Fenn College, Case Institute of Technology, and Dyke College. The center of Catholic life for the twelve thousand part-time and six thousand full-time students in these four institutions who live at home is Newman Hall on the Reserve-Case campus.

The situation at Wayne University has been carefully developed over a long period of years and doubtless serves as a fair model for most of the city situations. The large majority of the students (as in most municipal colleges and universities) are day students only and live at home. In Wayne University the students enjoy the Newman Foundation as a place for relaxation and study between classes and at the noon hour. Most of the Newman Foundation courses are scheduled at the noon hour, particularly on Tuesdays and Thursdays. Snacks are available and the first twenty minutes are devoted to lecture and the rest of the time to free and open discussion. The director of the Newman Club at Wayne has for many years been Father Maguire whose excellent article in *America* recently is quoted in another chapter. (See Chapter 3.)

Many Newman clubs throughout the country have specialized activities other than carrying on the personal counseling of the Catholic students by the priests in charge and the offering of Mass and administering the sacraments. These specialized extra activities, which vary in different institutions, may include the presentation of plays, public lectures by members of the faculty or from outside the college or university, and the publication of a periodical by the Newman Club.

In at least many Catholic parishes in the United States the youth of college age who are engaged in business and industry, busy on a job earning a living, whether they live at home or away from home, do not have available anything like the specialized religious service set up and operated for the benefit of youth which is offered by the Newman clubs.

In some colleges and universities there are fraternities and sororities limited to Catholic students only. Unquestionably these essentially social organizations in many cases have a decidedly good influence on their members, but, of course, reach only a limited number of students in any particular institution. Of late years in some institutions under the impact of current discussion of the undesirability of "divisive movements," separating people of one religion from those of another, and under the desire for total equality in institutions, there is found occasionally a desire to abolish all college fraternities and sororities. Some institutions have been seriously considering a regulation which would prohibit any college fraternity or sorority to have any admission requirements that mentioned race or religion. It seems evident that the principal motivating fact here has been the exclusion by some of the strong national fraternities of students from relatively small racial or religious background, such as Negroes, Jews, and (perhaps in some instances) Catholics. Of course this practice may be maintained without having any form of printed rule which anyone could point to and demand that it be repealed.

There is a difference of opinion among Catholic laymen experienced in secular education as to whether specifically Catholic fraternities and sororities are advisable. Against the doubtlessly good advice, example, and influence which these organizations give to some

Catholic students, there is a considerable feeling that in social matters the Catholic students should not set themselves apart from the rest of the institution, and that in so doing they lose one of the finest opportunities any American Catholics have for spreading the badly needed information concerning Catholics and their beliefs and practices.

There have been many striking instances of the improved attitude of many non-Catholics toward the Church and American Catholics that may be found today in secular institutions as compared to the attitude of non-Catholics of a decade ago. These changed attitudes, which are attributed principally to the free associations of Catholic and non-Catholic students, will doubtless exercise a strong influence on the relations of these non-Catholic students with their Catholic fellow citizens in the future. This seems to many of the Catholic members of secular faculties to be a more desirable contribution to Catholicism in America than is the limited influence of the fraternity and sorority on its members.

High praise for the work of the Newman clubs and their chaplains is substantially universal among Catholics experienced in secular education.

One such commentator emphasizes one aspect of the opportunity which all students inevitably have in this situation: "We are living and working here on a religious frontier. You can't any more keep from representing our faith among your friends than a candle can keep its light from penetrating the darkness." And he reminds the Catholic students of the Newman clubs that little candles shine a lot further in the dark than they do in the sunlight.

He does not expect the students to deliver lectures or enter formal debates with their fellow students on morals and religion, but he emphasizes what seems to me to be universally true in secular education, viz., that it is the daily contacts, the personal attitudes and habits, the casual conversations that are important and effective. The chance remark in classroom either by student or teacher, or in conversation around the fireplace or the dinner table, or on the street, or in the bleachers, demonstrates the lack of understanding and the opportunity for furnishing information. Such uninformed remarks can be answered effectively by any Catholic student—if he knows the answer and offers it courteously and with good humor. If the Catholic student does not know the answer, he can look it up, ask the chaplain (if there is one), get a pamphlet, write a note, or mention it the next time he has a good opportunity.

In this activity it is not necessary to quarrel with people or to offend them. In my experience, most of them are happy to be given, or to be directed to, accurate information. They do not oppose it; they welcome it. But someone has to offer it to them—someone who has the information and knows how to present it properly.

What is needed in the student body of the great secular institutions are not more Catholics, but more Catholics who are much better trained before they come into secular education in Catholic doctrine and Catholic history. Catholics who have the knowledge, will, and ability to spread information can help their fellow students (and sometimes their teachers) to some easily grasped aspects of Catholic doctrine, history, and program. Concerning these matters, many of the students and teachers know almost nothing, or worse yet, have been elaborately misinformed at someone's substantial profit.

In the spring of 1955, in a rather small group of Catholic educators from both Catholic and secular institutions, Archbishop Ritter of St. Louis said that he believed that Catholic schools ought to operate in very close cooperation with the state universities. Not only the heads of Catholic schools, but all organizations and persons in the Catholic Church should realize that state universities belong to the Catholics just as much as to the Protestants, the Jews, the secularists, the agnostics, or the atheists. The fact that Catholic influence in some of them is so much less than it should be in proportion to the Catholics in the population which owns and supports them is in large part the responsibility of the Catholics.

Apparently no accurate survey has ever been made of the number of Catholic students in the secular institutions at different levels. However, I have been furnished the numbers in some of the public colleges and universities. Some of the larger state universities have well over two thousand Catholic students each year. The largest precise figure I have is two thousand six hundred for a state university, and the smallest is three hundred. I have figures for some public colleges that go well over one thousand. In the large private non-Catholic universities the Catholic student body varies from none or very few to some thousands, and in the private colleges from none to a number of hundreds.

I know of no Catholic teacher or chaplain in a secular institution who is trying to get more Catholic students to enter secular education. The discussion of the desirability of more graduates of Catholic colleges entering secular graduate schools for advanced degrees, *for special reasons,* may perhaps be considered an exception to this statement (see Chapter 5). Almost unanimously they say that those who do go to secular institutions should be much better prepared.

One of the most effective chaplains I have ever known recently wrote:

Frankly, I would not wish to see more Catholic boys to enter ———. BUT I would like to do all I can to see that only fine Catholics . . . enter here. A non-sectarian institution is no place for a half-baked Catholic. . . . I have a thesis that I think I can pretty well establish that "No boy loses the Faith at ———." I can show that if he is a casualty, he never really had the Faith in the first place. You can't lose something you haven't had. And in any of the cases that have come to my attention in the last 6 years, I have found that the lad really didn't know what he was giving up and never really had the Faith in the first place.

One chaplain speaks of the boys who "get all fouled up morally" in high school or college and who can be brought back to religious and moral life in college. The number of Catholic youth, whether in school or not, who drop out of the Church in some communities, with little attention paid to them (either before or after their lapses), would probably surprise some of the bishops if they had the exact figures. Any of these young men who go to college will almost certainly go to a non-Catholic college, and some of them, I happen to know, after getting such attention from the Catholic chaplain as they have not before known, return to the Church.

Some people seem to assume that the primary objectives of the organization of Newman clubs, and assigning of chaplains to serve them, are to attract more Catholic students to secular institutions, or to make converts, or both. Neither assumption is true. The chief purpose is to assist in developing the moral and religious life of the current Catholic students. Obviously the presence on a particular campus of a strong Newman Club, with a competent chaplain to serve it, pleases many Catholic parents, and is doubtless a contributing factor to the decision of some Catholic students to apply for admission to such an institution. Obviously, also, the availability of a relatively young, approachable, personable priest who is always ready to answer questions, give explanations, and discuss disturbing personal problems, is an opportunity that many young people (especially those who are living in the stimulating atmosphere of a good college) will gladly make the most of. This leads inevitably, in colleges and universities as elsewhere, to a number of conversions to the Catholic faith. But they also occur in all sorts of communities.

Recently I spent a week end with a friend from school days in Canandaigua, now for many years pastor of the only Catholic parish in a small Midwestern city. On Saturday evening a young priest, Father X, from a near-by city, who had been a dinner guest, remarked to our host, "Monsignor, this is the first evening I have ever been in your house on which you had no appointments for instructing would-be converts to the Church." The reply was, "Well, Father X, I did have some, but I postponed them, because I wanted this evening for us three alone." Father X was a graduate of one of the secular institutions in which I had been a teacher, and I had told my old friend that I would like to meet this young priest whose story he had told me. Father X had been the pastor of a Protestant church in the same small city, and he and the Monsignor had been cordial friends for some time. One evening the young Protestant minister called at the Catholic rectory to announce that he wanted to join the Catholic Church. A year later the Monsignor received him into the Church; in a few years he was ordained and said his first Mass in the Monsignor's church.

I learned that evening that my boyhood friend had spent part of most of his evenings for many years in talking to prospective converts who came to him seeking information and instruction. It appears that when such a counselor is easily available anywhere there will be many converts. The records of many parishes, of such institutions as the Paulist Information Centers, and the replies to the advertisements of the Knights of Columbus, all testify to this.

There are inevitably quite a number of conversions wherever there are well-qualified Catholic chaplains working. These are some of the remarks that have come to me recently from secular colleges and universities:

From a relatively small institution:

Over the last five years I know of about five who have lost their faith while here—there are probably a few more. During the same five years I received into the Church forty-one students.

From a Far Western state university:

We have over twenty converts a year from the student body . . . about 50% of those who take pre-marital instructions . . . turn Catholic.

From a large private university:

We average about 50 conversions a year.

From a large Midwestern university:

Last year we had 49 converts.

One Catholic chaplain in a large state university sent me the following tabulated information for the year 1954–55:

Catholic enrollment	2,100
Annual attendance at Mass	104,000
Annual Communions	36,000
Masses	1,200
Sermons	250
Newman Club	150
Daily Mass attendance	125
Choir	40
Mass Servers	20
Baptisms	71
Converts	30
Marriages (5 mixed)	23

One of the undoubted weaknesses of the Newman Club organization in many places is that it is a club which a member must deliberately choose to join and to which he must pay dues, much as he would in the case of a bridge club or a bowling club. The difference between the Newman Club and some other clubs is that all Catholic students are invited to join the Newman Club and do not have to be especially invited after a vote of the membership. In many places the Newman Club membership is only a fraction of the Catholic membership in the student body of the college. A very much better situation seems to obtain where all Catholics registered in the institution are automatically members of the Newman Club, and there are no dues—only voluntary offerings from the students as in the parishes to which they are accustomed. The Newman clubs and their chaplains will not have a full opportunity to exercise their influence effectively in the basic matter of the faith and morals of the students until there is such an arrangement in each institution.

This happy financial solution is brought about in some (probably most) places where it is in operation by the bishops of the dioceses who provide adequate Catholic centers to house the various activities of the Newman Clubs and usually to serve in part as the residence of the chaplain. In addition, as a rule, funds are solicited from Catholic alumni and from the parents of Catholic students. The better Catholic centers contain the chaplain's office, a chapel, a library and reading room, a lounge, and a large room, or small hall, for various kinds of meetings, lectures, dances, and social gatherings. The chapels are often too small, requiring six or seven Masses each Sunday, and as many as three daily Masses.

I know of no Catholic teachers or chaplains in secular education who do not approve this type of organization. It seems so obviously the only effective way in which the religious life of the majority of Catholics who are getting a college education can be served that an inevitable question to Catholic chaplains is, "Why don't you adopt the scheme?" And the inevitable answer is like the explanation of why there are no more Catholics in the Church's elementary and high schools: "We have neither the money nor the staff to care for all the Catholics, and we have to collect dues to get along at all."

In some places the Newman clubs are still suffering, in varying degrees, from the last smoldering of the opposition which flared up quite generally when the movement was first started. Many felt that the assignment of a chaplain by a bishop was a formal encouragement of anti-Catholic competition with the schools and colleges of the Church, and a tremendous danger to the Catholic faith of the students. This attitude has largely died out as the facts concerning the numbers who leave the Church apparently from the influences that they experienced in secular education became well known, from the graduates of secular colleges who entered the priesthood, and from the reports, formal and informal, of Catholic chaplains and Catholic teachers in secular institutions.

However, there are chaplains and Catholic faculty members who express the wish that some of the bishops were more interested in learning accurately the circumstances surrounding these large groups of young Catholics in their dioceses, and in taking steps to improve the conditions. On the other hand some chaplains express great enthusiasm for the attention and the support, financial and other, which their bishops give to the work of the Newman clubs. Some of the Catholic faculty members deplore the type of priest which a few bishops select for assignment as Newman Club chaplains. Probably all Catholics who have known many members of the priesthood will agree that priests, like other men, differ widely in personal traits and tastes and social adaptability. Some are good "labor priests," others good "water-front priests," rural priests, urban priests, teachers, or missionaries. The sort that are good "Newman Club priests" should be deeply interested in young people, and able to mingle easily, comfortably, and with real enjoyment with the members of college and university faculties, most of whom are not Catholics. Most commentators seem to think that their bishops have made excellent selections for chaplains, but some wish a different selection had been made, and some even fear that an individual bishop does not pay enough attention to the matter. In a few instances some faculty members have said that a poor choice for appointment as a chaplain has practically wrecked the Newman Club.

Probably more important, on account of its greater "coverage," is the lack of cooperation with the Newman Club chaplains of the home parish pastors of *some* of the students, and of the parents of *many* of the students. It cannot be overemphasized that Newman clubs served by carefully chosen chaplains offer the best opportunity the Church has for providing for the religious training of the majority of the American Catholics of the future who will have a college education.

8

To the Stockholders

On the combined authority of the *Official Catholic Directory* and the Confraternity of Christian Doctrine, there were last year approximately 5,226,707 Catholics being educated in non-Catholic institutions under the American flag, and approximately 4,308,606 in Catholic schools, colleges, and universities. Since most of these in non-Catholic education are unquestionably in public education, it seems fair to assume that at least 4,000,000 are now getting their formal education in institutions conducted by the public authorities. If the prophecies in the Catholic press of recent months are correct, this figure will grow steadily in the immediate future. So long as the private schools and agencies of higher education obey the constitutions and laws of the country the American public is not responsible for the administration of these institutions; but the American public, the whole American public, owns the public educational system, and is wholly responsible for what happens, and what does not happen, in public education.

The individual American citizens are the stockholders who choose the directors, who exercise the immediate administrative control of the enterprise; they adopt the constitutional provisions which authorize public education, and elect the legislators who write the educational laws, and the executives who enforce them.

American Catholics own about a one-fifth interest in the business of public education. They, therefore, have the responsibilities, and the opportunities, for profit (or loss) comparable to the responsibilities and opportunities of a block of one fifth of the holders of the common stock in a vast corporation in which there is no preferred stock. All groups have, or should have, the same objective for public education—the best possible education for the great majority of the future stockholders of America itself. It seems to follow from all this that American Catholics, and some others, should repudiate the idea that the Catholic one-fifth of the stockholders do not have, or should not have, either voice or vote in the affairs of their corporation in which they have invested a large part of the future of their children.

The fair-minded American public, overwhelmingly and actively Protestant at the time, ended the conduct of the public schools as essentially Protestant schools at public expense in the last half of the last century. Apparently, however, there still persists among a vocal and effective minority of both Catholics and non-Catholics the theory that the public education system belongs to Protestants or secularists, and that Catholics should keep out of it and mind their own business.

No minority in industry, politics, or education should attempt to dictate to the majority, or to take over control, or to stop the functioning of the enterprise by devices aimed at slowing down or wrecking the machinery. Trying to improve the processes and the output by explanation, evidence, and argument in directors' meetings, or in choosing the directors, will probably bring any minority better dividends than the negative technique of "throwing monkey wrenches."

The Catholic stockholders in public education when they are a minority (like the minority stockholders in other organizations) should know the problems and the proposed solutions, should be present at all stockholders' meetings, and should participate fully and frankly on equal terms with members of the majority in all discussions. Probably relevant to some of the deliberations of general stockholders' meetings is the fact that, on the combined authority of the *Catholic Directory* and the U.S. Department of Health, Education, and Welfare, the Catholic system of education saves the

American taxpayers approximately $5,595,540 each school day of the school year. I am confident that the great majority of non-Catholic stockholders in public education will welcome the activity of the Catholic minority, in information, advice, arguments, and votes, and will in most instances accept it for what it is worth to the whole enterprise.

When and where the Catholics are a majority of the stockholders in any area or unit in public education, they must be meticulous in granting to all minority groups the full freedom in discussion, and in participation in the affairs of the organization, which they desire for themselves—even though in isolated cases they have failed to get all that they properly deserved. Only so can they achieve the best in the American way as found in American constitutions, laws, and traditions.

Doubtless Professor Schlesinger, as quoted by Father John Tracy Ellis in an earlier reference in this book, is quite right in holding that anti-Catholic bias is the most persistent prejudice in American history, and is still with us; but in our country it is today a weak and dying descendent of its manifestations of only a few decades ago. The Know Nothings, and the Ku Klux Klan of the bedsheets and the fiery crosses, have only puny successors in present-day America. True, we have with us even now a small and busy modern sort of Klan that can read and write—and speak; but these contemporary Knights of The Invisible Empire seem not so much interested in "converting the benighted Catholics from their superstitions," as in making money by selling their books and speeches to the ignorant and gullible whose simple emotions can be easily titillated.

If public education in our country is ever to serve the interest of all of America's pluralistic society, it must welcome the participation of all American groups regardless of their size, and must treat all fairly with no discrimination on the basis of religion, race, or national origin. However, before such beneficent results can be realized, all minorities (including the Catholic) must show a complete willingness to cooperate cordially, and to work frankly through all appropriate channels to influence public education to move in the direction in which they think it should go—just as all other groups do. As responsible stockholders they can do no less; and they are responsible stockholders whether they like it or not.

Bibliography

[The page numbers following each item give the pages *in this book* on which the listed item is referred to.]

A. BOOKS

ATWATER, DONALD. *The Catholic Dictionary*. New York: Macmillan, 1943. (p. 87)

BEALE, HOWARD K. *History of Freedom of Teaching*. New York: Scribners, 1941. (pp. 45, 86)

BILLINGTON, RAY ALLEN. *The Protestant Crusade*. New York: Macmillan, 1938; Rinehart and Company, 1952. (pp. 45, 86)

BLANSHARD, PAUL. *American Freedom and Catholic Power*. Boston: Beacon Press, 1949. (p. 34)

CONANT, JAMES B. *Education and Liberty*. Cambridge: Harvard University Press, 1953. (p. 11)

CURTI, MERLE. *Social Ideas of American Educators*. New York: Scribners, 1935. (pp. 45, 86)

DAWSON, JOSEPH MARTIN. *America's Way in Church, State, and Society*. New York: Macmillan, 1953. (p. 123)

ELDERKIN, GEORGE W. *The Roman Catholic Problem*. New York: Vantage Press, 1954. (p. 34)

GANNON, ROBERT I., S.J. *"The Hedge Master"* in *After Black Coffee*. New York: McMullen, 1947. (p. 87)

JOHNSON, F. ERNEST (ed.). *American Education and Religion*. New York: Harpers, 1952. (pp. 113 ff.)

MOEHLMAN, CONRAD H. *The Wall of Separation between Church and State*. Boston: Beacon Press, 1951. (p. 123)

MYERS, GUSTAVUS. *History of Bigotry in the United States*. New York: Random House, 1943. (p. 85)

NICHOLS, JAMES H. *Democracy and the Church*. Philadelphia: Westminster Press, 1951. (p. 34)

O'BRIEN, REV. JOHN A. *Catholics and Scholarship*. Huntington, Ind.: Our Sunday Visitor, 1939. (pp. 62–63, 77, 79, 91, 95, 98, 100)

O'NEILL, J. M. *Catholicism and American Freedom*. New York: Harpers, 1949. (p. 16)

O'NEILL, J. M. *Religion and Education under the Constitution.* New York: Harpers, 1949. (pp. 125, 135)

PFEFFER, LEO. *Church, State, and Freedom.* Boston: Beacon Press, 1953. (p. 123)

PRITCHETT, C. HERMAN. *Civil Liberties and the Vinson Court.* Chicago: University of Chicago Press, 1954. (p. 187)

RAY, SISTER MARY AUGUSTINE. *American Opinion of Catholicism in the Eighteenth Century.* New York: Columbia University Press, 1936. (p. 85)

ROMMEN, HEINRICH. *The State in Catholic Thought.* St. Louis: Herder Book Company, 1947. (p. 16)

SHUSTER, GEORGE N. *The Catholic Spirit in America.* New York: Dial Press, 1927. (p. 95)

B. PERIODICALS, PAMPHLETS, ARTICLES, ESSAYS

CASTLE, LATHAM, quoted in the *Catholic Transcript.* (p. 110)

Catholic Directory. New York: P. J. Kenedy & Sons, 1955. (pp. 1–5)

Catholic Transcript (Hartford). (pp. 6, 28)

Christian Century, The (Chicago). (p. 123)

CURLING, ARCHBISHOP R. J. "Criticism of Conant Doctrine," *Saturday Review* (May 3, 1952). (p. 13)

Current Expenditures per Pupil in Public School Systems (U. S. Dept. of Health, Education and Welfare, Circulars No. 436 and 438.) Washington, D.C.: Government Printing Office, 1955. (p. 4)

DAWSON, CHRISTOPHER. "The Challenge of Secularism," *Catholic World* (February, 1956). (p. 103)

DE LAUNAY, GREGORY F. X. "Catholic Teachers at Secular Colleges," *Catholic World* (New York: Paulist Press, February, 1956). (p. 104)

ELLIS, REV. JOHN TRACY. "The American Catholic and the Intellectual Life," *Thought* (Autumn, 1955). (pp. 83 ff.)

FLEEGE, URBAN H. *The Tablet* (Brooklyn, June 5, 1954). (pp. 28–29)

FOSTER, O. D. "Religious Census of State Universities and Colleges," *Christian Education* (Chicago: Council of Church Boards of Education, June, 1921). (p. 63)

HEELEY, ALLAN V. "Criticism of Conant Doctrine," *Saturday Review* (May 3, 1952). (p. 13)

HERZFELD, K. F. "Religion and Scholarship," *Commonweal* (March 19, 1929). (p. 95)

JOHNSON, F. ERNEST. "Religion in Education," *Current Religious Thought* (Oberlin, February, 1950). (p. 119)

KARGAN, A. "Financial Problems of Catholic Colleges," *America* (New York, April 11, 1953). (p. 24)

LE BUFFE, REV. X., S.J., quoted by Rev. John A. O'Brien, "Catholics and Scholarship," *The Tabloid* (New York, February 1, 1935). (p. 79)

MAGUIRE, JAMES J. "Another Look at Subversion of Faith," *America* (New York, December 4, 1954). (pp. 39, 42)

McCLURE, LOIS V. "Weekday Religious Education at the High School Level," reprinted from *Religious Education* (Chicago: National Council of Churches of Christ, January-February, 1952). (p. 110)

McCREADY, DR. EDWARD. "On the McCollum Decision," *The Pilot* (Boston, January 22, 1955). (p. 121)

McMANUS, MSGR. W. E., quoted in *The Catholic Mind* (New York, December, 1954). (pp. 18–21, 27, 28)

MILLER, J. HILLIS. "Religion in a State University," *American Education and Religion*. (p. 114)

Monitor, The (San Francisco). (p. 95)

MURRAY, REV. JOHN COURTNEY. "Reversing the Secular Trend," *Thought* (March, 1949). (p. 60)

MUTTKOWSKI, RICHARD. "What Is Research," *America* (June 29, 1929). (p. 95)

Newman Club in American Education. Washington: National Association of Newman Club Chaplains, 1953. (p. 146)

O'BRIEN, REV. JOHN A. "Developing Catholic Scholars," *America* (New York, June 7, 1947). (p. 101)

O'NEILL, J. M. "Education and Liberty," *Social Order* (St. Louis, Summer, 1953). (p. 13)

——. "Religious Education and American Democracy," *Vital Speeches of the Day* (New York, May 15, 1952). (p. 13)

——. "Scholarship and Emotional Voltage," *Thought* (New York, Winter, 1951–52). (p. 35)

PIKE, THE VERY REV. JAMES A., in the *New York Times,* April 12, 1952. (p. 13)

Pilot, The (Boston). (p. 6)

"Public Aid to Parochial Education," *Harvard Law School Forum* (Cambridge, Mass., March 16, 1951). (p. 50)

Public Education and the Future of America. Washington: National Education Association, 1955. (pp. 7, 42 ff.)

Register, The (Denver, Col.). (p. 23)

Released Time (pamphlet) (Department of Weekday Religious Education.) Chicago: National Council of Churches of Christ, undated. (p. 110)

SHUSTER, GEORGE N. "Have We Any Scholars?" *America* (New York, August 15, 1925). (p. 95)

Saturday Review, The (New York). (pp. 12, 13)

SONTAG, RAYMOND J. "Catholic Undergraduates in Non-Catholic Colleges," *Thought* (New York, March, 1949). (p. 140)

STRODE, RALPH H. "Subversion of Faith by Intellectuals," *America* (New York, October 9, 1954). (p. 37)

Tabloid Scientist (New York: Fordham University). (p. 79)

TAYLOR, HUGH STOTT, essay in *Born Catholics.* New York: Sheed and Ward, 1954. (p. 57)

———. "Catholic Scholars in Secular Universities," *Thought* (New York, March, 1949). (pp. 60, 82)

THAYER, DR. VIVIAN. "An Experimentalist Position," *American Education and Religion.* (p. 116)

United States Law Week (Washington, April 29, 1952). (p. 134)

YANCEY, REV. P. H., S.J., quoted by Rev. John A. O'Brien, "Catholics and Scholarship," *The Tabloid* (New York, February 1, 1935). (p. 81)

C. LAW CASES

Adamson v. California. 312 U.S. 46 (1947). (p. 137)

Doremus v. Board of Education. 342 U.S. 429 (1952). (p. 173)

McCollum v. Board of Education. 333 U.S. 203 (1948). (pp. 1, 15, 47, 108, 110–111, 120–123, 125, 127–130)

Pierce v. Society of Sisters. 268 U.S. 510 (1923). (pp. 44, 133)

Reynolds v. U.S. 98 U.S. 145 (1879). (p. 135)

Wolf v. Colorado. 338 U.S. 25 (1949). (p. 137)
Zorach v. Clauson. 343 U.S. 306 (1952). (pp. 109, 120–123, 127–130)

Index

[Publications cited in this book are not included in this index. See note at head of bibliography preceding.]

Date Due

FEB 5 '57	MY 19 59	JY 6 '67	
FEB 1 4	JY 24 '59	JY 20 '67	
FEB 1 4 '57		AP 10 '68	
	DE 16 59		
APR 1 1 '57	AG 3 '60		
APR 1 0 '57			
APR 3 0 '57	DE 15 '60		
APR 3 0 '57	MR 1 61		
JY 20 '57	MR 17 '61		
OC 6 '57	MR 23 '61		
OC 10 '57	AP 11 61		
OC 24 '57	JE 28 61		
NO 7 '57	Reserve		
NO 2 2 '57	6-20 61		
DE 10 '57	Bro. Julius		
DE 17 '57	DE 13 '82		
FE 27 '58	JA 18 '63		
MR 11 '58	MY 20 35		
MR 27 '58	AP 6 '66		

NO. 340   PRINTED IN U.S.A.   BECKLEY - CARDY CO.